D0443832

The True Solitude

SELECTIONS FROM THE WRITINGS OF

The True Solitude

Thomas Merton

SELECTED BY DEAN WALLEY

HALLMARK EDITIONS

Contents

THOMAS MERTON lived as a Trappist monk for just over half his life, observing a rule of silence, prayers and contemplation. How is it, then, that his name is known all over the world, that thousands mourned his death in Bangkok on December 10, 1968? Perhaps the twenty-six years he lived before entering the monastery provide some explanation of the kind of man and the kind of monk he was.

He was born in Prades, France, in 1915, to a New Zealand father and American mother, both of them artists. His education was cosmopolitan—France, England, and America. Columbia gave him a B.A. and an M.A., and a friendship there with a Buddhist monk was instrumental, oddly enough, in his becoming a Roman Catholic. For awhile he taught English and wrote novels and poetry. In his twenty-sixth year he became convinced that he required a closer union with God than he could achieve in everyday life. On December 10, 1941, he entered the Abbey of Gethsemani, in Kentucky.

He expected to sacrifice all his dreams of becoming a successful author. But his superiors saw that he had a talent for communicating with others and that he should use it. In 1949, his autobiography, *The Seven Storey Mountain*, was published and was an immediate and international best-seller. Thomas Merton was a celebrity—not an easy role for a contemplative monk. There followed some thirty or more books of prose and poetry, each one bringing more readers and correspondence from all over the world. People sought his advice, his help, his encouragement, his spiritual direction. His gift of identification was so great that to each one he became the closest of friends. His early books were of a spiritual nature but in later years he wrote of matters that weighed upon him—war and its futility, racial injustice, the increasing violence of American life.

In 1966, he retired to a small hermitage in the woods near the Abbey. He did not shut out the world, for the years had taught him that there must not be a stone curtain behind which the monk could hide. It is the life at this hermitage that he describes in this book in "Day of a Stranger."

In the fall of 1968, he set out on a trip to Asia, the fulfillment of a dream. In India he met and talked at length with the Dalai Lama and many Buddhist monks. And in Bangkok, after giving a widely applauded speech to a group of Asian Abbots, he died of heart failure, perhaps caused by an accident with an electric fan in his room. There seemed so much he still had to say, so much good still to do, and yet, to those who had been aware, through the years, of his struggle to know God and himself, it was not a tragic death. He had come to the end of his search.

Naomi Burton/York, Maine/May 8, 1969

The True Solitude

The average Trappist monastery is a quiet, out-of-the-way place—usually somewhere in France—occupied by a community of seventy or eighty men who lead a silent energetic life consecrated entirely to God. It is a life of prayer and of penance, of liturgy, study, and manual labor. The monks are supposed to exercise no exterior ministry—no preaching, teaching, or the rest. The only teaching done by the monks is confined to classes of theology and philosophy within the monastery itself—classes attended by the young monks, or "scholastics," preparing for the priesthood.

The life is physically hard, but the compensation for this hardship is interior peace. In any case, one soon becomes used to the hardships and finds that they are not so hard after all. Seven hours of sleep are normally enough. The monks' diet is extremely plain, but is ordinarily enough to keep a man healthy for long years, and monks traditionally die of old age. One soon gets used to sleeping on straw and boards. Most monks would find it difficult to sleep on a soft mattress, after their simple pallets.

The life is usually quiet. There is no conversation. The monks talk to their superiors or spiritual directors when necessary. In the average monastery, Trappist silence is an all-pervading thing that seeps into the very stones of the place and saturates the men who live there.

Farm labor is the monks' support, and the ordinary thing is for all the monks to work outdoors for five or six hours a day. When they are not working, or praying in choir, the monks devote their time to reading, meditation, contemplative prayer. The whole day is supposed eventually to become a prolonged prayer in which the monk remains united with God through all his occupations. This is the real purpose of the monastic life: a more or less habitual state of simple prayer and union with God which varies in intensity at different times of the day, which finds a particular and proper rhythm in the life of each individual, and which brings the soul of the monk at all times under the direct and intimate influence of God's action.

*T*oday, at work in the woods, I nearly cut off both my legs. The ax kept glancing off the felled pine tree I was supposed to be trimming. It flew at my knees like a fierce, bright-beaked bird and my guardian angel had a busy afternoon fencing with the blade to keep me on my two feet. The woods were wonderful.

*O*nce again, it seems to me that I ought to give up all desire for the lights and satisfactions that make me too pleased with myself at prayer. I should want nothing but to do all the ordinary things a monk has to do, regularly and properly, without any special thought of satisfaction in them.

I am thinking especially of Holy Communion. Today is a good day to think about it. Everything I came here to find seems to me to be concentrated in the twenty or thirty minutes of silent and happy absorption that follow Communion when I get a chance to make a thanksgiving that seems to me to be a thanksgiving. I like to remain alone and quiet after Mass. Then my mind is relaxed and my imagination is quiet and my will drowns in the attraction of a Love beyond understanding, beyond definite ideas.

Now it is evening. The frogs still sing. After the showers of rain around dinner time the sky cleared. All afternoon I sat on the bed rediscovering the meaning of contemplation —rediscovering God, rediscovering myself —and the office, and Scripture and everything.

It has been one of the most beautiful days I have ever known in my life, and yet I am not attached to that part of it either. Any pleasure or the contentment I may have got out of silence and solitude and freedom from all care does not matter. But I know that is the way I ought to be *living*: with my mind and senses silent, contact with the world of business and war and community troubles severed—not solicitous for anything high or low or far or near. Not pushing myself around with my own fancies or desires or projects—and not letting myself get hurried off my feet by excessive current of natural activity that flows through the universe with full force.

I ought to know, by now, that God uses everything that happens as a means to lead me into solitude. Every creature that enters my life, every instant of my days, will be designed to wound me with the realization of the world's insufficiency, until I become so detached that I will be able to find God alone in everything. Only then will all things bring me joy.

Even the consolations of prayer, lights in the intellect and sensible fervor in the will: everything that touches me burns me at least lightly. I cannot hold on to anything. The pain in all these things is the pledge of God's love for me, as long as I am as weak in the spirit as I still am. This pain is the promise of solitude.

Today I seem to be very much assured that solitude is indeed His will for me and that it is truly God Who is calling me into the desert. But this desert is not necessarily a geographical one. It is a solitude of heart in which created joys are consumed and reborn in God.

A priest must not put the salvation of souls above his own soul. There is no question of a choice like that. But he has to put God and the Mass before everything. He has the whole Church on his conscience, and he not only gives up his will in order to possess the virtue of obedience, he gives up his will in order to become an instrument for the salvation of the world and for the pure glory of God.

*I*t is in deep solitude that I find the gentleness with which I can truly love my brothers. The more solitary I am, the more affection I have for them. It is pure affection, and filled with reverence for the solitude of others. Solitude and silence teach me to love my brothers for what they are, not for what they say. Now it is no longer a question of dishonoring them by accepting their fictions, believing in their images of themselves which their weakness obliges them to compose, in the wan work of communication. Yet there will, it is true, always remain a dialectic between the words of men and their being. This will tell something about them we would not have realized if the words had not been there.

*T*enderness of the Epistle, austerity of the Gospel in this morning's Mass. Last night before Compline, out by the horsebarn, looking at the orchard and thinking about what Saint John of the Cross said about having in your heart the image of Christ crucified.

Confusion and fog pile up in your life, and then by the power of the Cross things once again are clear, and you know more about your wretchedness and you are grateful for another miracle.

*T*oday I was on as deacon at Benediction. The new sense of practicality did not extend to the ceremonies. I was in a fog, but very happy. All I could think about was picking up the Host. I was afraid the whole Church might come down on my head, because of what I used to be—as if that were not forgotten!

But God weighs scarcely anything at all.

Though containing more than the universe, He was so light that I nearly fell off the altar. He communicated all that lightness to my own spirit and when I came down I was so happy I had a hard time to keep myself from laughing out loud.

The blue elm tree near at hand and the light blue hills in the distance: the red bare clay where I am supposed to plant some shade trees: these are before me as I sit in the sun for a free half hour between direction and work. Tomorrow is Ash Wednesday and today, as I sit in the sun, big blue and purple fish swim past me in the darkness of my empty mind, this sea which opens within me as soon as I close my eyes. Delightful darkness, delightful sun, shining on a world which, for all I care, has already ended.

It does not occur to me to wonder whether

we will ever transplant the young maples from the wood, yonder, to this bare leveled patch—the place where the old horsebarn once stood. It does not occur to me to wonder how everything here came to be transformed. I sit on a cedar log half chewed by some novice's blunt ax, and do not reflect on the plans I have made for this place of prayer, because they do not matter. They will happen when they will happen. The hills are as pure as jade in the distance. God is in His transparent world, but He is too sacred to be mentioned, too holy to be observed. I sit in silence. The big deep fish are purple in my sea.

*E*vening: cold winter wind along the walls of the chapel. Not howling, not moaning, not dismal. Can there be anything mournful about wind? It is innocent, and without sorrow. It has no regrets. Wind is a strong child enjoying his play, amazed at his own strength, gentle, inexhaustible, and pure. He burnishes the dry snow, throwing clouds of it against the building. The wind has no regrets. The chapel is very cold. Two die-hard novices remain there alone, kneeling both upright, very still, no longer even pretending to enjoy or to understand anything.

There is no true solitude except interior solitude. And interior solitude is not possible for anyone who does not accept his true place in relation to other men. There is no true peace possible for the man who still imagines that some accident of talent or grace or virtue segregates him from other men and places him above them.

God does not give us graces or talents or virtues for ourselves alone. We are members one of another and everything that is given to one member is given for the whole body. I do not wash my feet to make them more beautiful than my face.

When the Dalai Lama was young, still a boy, he was lonely in his palace, the Potala, and would walk on the roof looking through field glasses down upon the houses of his subjects to see if they were having parties, and in order to watch them enjoying themselves. They, in their turn, would hide themselves and hold parties out of his sight, so as not to sadden him still more.

I am content that these pages show me to be what I am—noisy, full of the racket of my imperfections and passions, and the wide open wounds left by my sins. Full of my own emptiness. Yet, ruined as my house is, You live there!

*T*here is only one true flight from the world; it is not an escape from conflict, anguish and suffering, but the flight from disunity and separation, to unity and peace in the love of other men.

What is the "world" that Christ would not pray for, and of which He said that His disciples were in it but not of it? The world is the unquiet city of those who live for themselves and are therefore divided against one another in a struggle that cannot end, for it will go on eternally in hell. It is the city of those who are fighting for possession of limited things and for the monopoly of goods and pleasures that cannot be shared by all.

But if you try to escape from this world merely by leaving the city and hiding yourself in solitude, you will only take the city with you into solitude; and yet you can be entirely out of the world while remaining in the midst of it, if you let God set you free from your own selfishness and if you live for love alone.

For the flight from the world is nothing else but the flight from self-concern. And the man who locks himself up in private with his own selfishness has put himself into a position where the evil within him will either possess him like a devil or drive him out of his head.

That is why it is dangerous to go into solitude merely because you like to be alone.

How the valley awakes. At two-fifteen in the morning there are no sounds except in the monastery: the bells ring, the office begins. Outside, nothing, except perhaps a bullfrog saying "Om" in the creek or in the guest-house pond. Some nights he is in Samadhi;

there is not even "Om." The mysterious and uninterrupted whooping of the whippoorwill begins about three, these mornings. He is not always near. Sometimes there are two whooping together, perhaps a mile away in the woods in the east.

The first chirps of the waking day birds mark the *"point vierge"* of the dawn under a sky as yet without real light, a moment of awe and inexpressible innocence, when the Father in perfect silence opens their eyes. They begin to speak to Him, not with fluent song, but with an awakening question that is their dawn state, their state at the *"point vierge."* Their condition asks if it is time for them to "be." He answers "yes." Then, they one by one wake up, and become birds. They manifest themselves as birds, beginning to sing. Presently they will be fully themselves, and will even fly.

Meanwhile, the most wonderful moment of the day is that when creation in its innocence asks permission to "be" once again, as it did on the first morning that ever was.

All wisdom seeks to collect and manifest itself at that blind sweet point. Man's wisdom does not succeed, for we are fallen into self-mastery and cannot ask permission of anyone. We face our mornings as men of undaunted purpose. We know the time and we dictate terms. We are in a position to dictate terms, we suppose: We have a clock that proves we are right from the very start. We know what time it is. We are in touch with the hidden inner laws. We will say in advance what kind of day it has to be. Then if necessary we will take steps to make it meet our requirements.

For the birds there is not a time that they tell, but the virgin point between darkness and light, between nonbeing and being. You can tell yourself the time by their waking, if you are experienced. But that is your folly, not theirs. Worse folly still if you think they are telling you something you might consider useful—that it is, for example, four o'clock.

So they wake: first the catbirds and cardinals and some that I do not know. Later the song sparrows and wrens. Last of all the doves and crows.

The waking of crows is most like the waking of men: querulous, noisy, raw.

Here is an unspeakable secret: paradise is all around us and we do not understand. It is wide open. The sword is taken away, but we do not know it: we are off "one to his farm and another to his merchandise." Lights on. Clocks ticking. Thermostats working. Stoves cooking. Electric shavers filling radios with static. "Wisdom," cries the dawn deacon, but we do not attend.

A spring morning alone in the woods. Sunrise: the enormous yolk of energy spreading as if to take over the entire sky. After that: the ceremonies of the birds feeding in the wet grass. The meadowlark, feeding and singing. Then the quiet, totally silent, dry, sun-drenched midmorning of spring, under the climbing sun. April is not the cruelest month. Not in Kentucky. It was hard to say Psalms. Attention would get carried away in the vast blue arc of the sky, trees, hills, grass, and all things. How absolutely central is the truth that we are first of all *part of nature*, though we are a very special part, that which is conscious of God. In solitude, one is entirely surrounded by beings which perfectly obey God. This leaves only one place open for me, and if I occupy that place then I, too, am fulfilling His will. The place nature "leaves open" belongs to the conscious one, the one who is aware, who sees all this as a unity, who offers it all to God in praise, joy, thanks. To me, these are not "spiritual acts" or special virtues, but rather the simple, normal, obvious functions of man, without which it is hard to see how he can be human. Obviously he has learned to live in another dimension, that which one may call "the world" in the sense of a realm of man and his machines, in which each individual is closed in upon himself and his own ideas—clear or unclear—his own desires, his own concerns, and no one pays any attention to the whole. One has to be alone, under the sky, before everything falls into place and one finds his own place in the midst of it all.

It is not Christianity, far from it, that separates man from the cosmos, the world of sense and of nature. On the contrary, it is man's own technocratic and self-centered "worldliness" which is in reality a falsification and a perversion of natural perspectives, which separates him from the reality of creation, and enables him to act out his fantasies as a little autonomous god, seeing and judging everything in relation to himself.

We have to have the humility first of all to realize ourselves as part of nature. Denial of this results only in madnesses and cruelties. One can be part of nature, surely, without being Lady Chatterly's lover.

It was one good morning. A return in spirit to the first morning of the world.

*T*he soul of man, left to its own natural level, is a potentially lucid crystal left in darkness. It is perfect in its own nature, but it lacks something that it can only receive from outside and above itself. But when the light shines in it, it becomes in a manner transformed into light and seems to lose its nature in the splendor of a higher nature, the nature of the light that is in it.

*D*espair is the absolute extreme of self-love. It is reached when a man deliberately turns his back on all help from anyone else in order to taste the rotten luxury of knowing himself to be lost.

In every man there is hidden some root of despair because in every man there is pride that vegetates and springs weeds and rank

flowers of self-pity as soon as our own resources fail us. But because our own resources
inevitably fail us, we are all more or less sub-
ject to discouragement and to despair.

Despair is the ultimate development of a
pride so great and so stiff-necked that it se-
lects the absolute misery of damnation rather
than accept happiness from the hands of God
and thereby acknowledge that He is above us
and that we are not capable of fulfilling our
destiny by ourselves.

*But a man who is truly humble cannot de-
spair, because in the humble man there is no
longer any such thing as self-pity.*

*O*ur discovery of God is, in a way, God's discovery of us. We cannot go to heaven to find Him because we have no way of knowing where heaven is or what it is. He comes down from heaven and finds us. He looks at us from the depths of His own infinite actuality, which is everywhere, and His seeing us gives us a superior reality in which we also discover Him. We only know Him in so far as we are known by Him, and our contemplation of Him is a participation of His contemplation of Himself.

We become contemplatives when God discovers Himself in us.

At that moment, the point of our contact with Him opens out and we pass through the center of our own souls, and enter eternity.

*D*o not look for rest in any pleasure, because you were not created for pleasure: you were created for Joy. And if you do not know the difference between pleasure and joy you have not yet begun to live.

You cannot be a man of faith unless you know how to doubt. You cannot believe in God unless you are capable of questioning the authority of prejudice, even though that prejudice may seem to be religious. Faith is not blind conformity to a prejudice—a "pre-judgment." It is a decision, a judgment that is fully and deliberately taken in the light of a truth that cannot be proven. It is not merely the acceptance of a decision that has been made by somebody else.

Winter morning, pale sunshine. White smoke rises up in the valley, against the light, slowly taking on animal forms, against the dark wall of wooded hills behind. Menacing and peaceful forms. Probably this is the smoke of brush fires in the hollow. It might be the smoke of a burning house. Probably not a burning house. Big animal against the blue wall of the hill, a lion of smoke changing into a smoke bear. Cold, quiet morning, the watch ticks on the table, nothing happens. The smoke dragon rises, claws the winter sunlight, and vanishes over the hills.

*I*t is a glorious destiny to be a member of the human race, though it is a race dedicated to many absurdities and one which makes many terrible mistakes: yet, with all that, God Himself gloried in becoming a member of the human race. A member of the human race! To think that such a commonplace realization should suddenly seem like news that one holds the winning ticket in a cosmic sweepstake.

*O*nly the man who has had to face despair is really convinced that he needs mercy. Those who do not want mercy never seek it. It is better to find God on the threshold of despair than to risk our lives in a complacency that has never felt the need of forgiveness. A life that is without problems may literally be more hopeless than one that always verges on despair.

*P*rayer is inspired by God in the depth of our nothingness. It is the movement of trust, of gratitude, of adoration, or of sorrow that places us before God, seeing both Him and ourselves in the light of His infinite truth, and moves us to ask Him for the mercy, the spiritual strength, the material help that we all need. The man whose prayer is so pure that he never asks God for anything does not know who God is, and does not know who he is himself: for he does not know his own need of God.

All true prayer somehow confesses our absolute dependence on the Lord of life and death. It is, therefore, a deep and vital contact with Him Whom we know not only as Lord but as Father. It is when we pray truly that we really *are*. Our being is brought to a high perfection by this, which is one of its most perfect activities. When we cease to pray, we tend to fall back into nothingness. True, we continue to exist. But since the main reason for our existence is the knowledge and love of God, when our conscious contact with Him is severed we sleep or we die.

*W*hat is serious to men is often very trivial in the sight of God. What in God might appear to us as "play" is perhaps what He Himself takes most seriously. At any rate the Lord plays and diverts Himself in the garden of His creation, and if we could let go of our own obsession with what we think is the meaning of it all, we might be able to hear His call and follow Him in His mysterious, cosmic dance. We do not have to go very far to catch echoes of that game, and of that dancing. When we are alone on a starlit night; when by chance we see the migrating birds in autumn descending on a grove of junipers to rest and eat; when we see children in a moment when they are really children; when we know love in our own hearts; or when, like the Japanese poet Basho, we hear an old frog land in a quiet pond with a solitary splash—at such times the awakening, the turning inside out of all values, the "newness," the emptiness and the purity of vision that make themselves evident, provide a glimpse of the cosmic dance.

For the world and time are the dance of the Lord in emptiness. The silence of the spheres is the music of a wedding feast. The more we persist in misunderstanding the phenomena of life, the more we analyze them out into strange finalities and complex purposes of our own, the more we involve ourselves in sadness, absurdity and despair. But it does not matter much, because no despair of ours can alter the reality of things, or stain the joy of the cosmic dance which is always there. Indeed, we are in the midst of it, and it is in the midst of us, for it beats in our very blood, whether we want it to or not.

Yet the fact remains that we are invited to forget ourselves on purpose, cast our awful solemnity to the winds and join in the general dance.

*P*rayer and love are learned in the hour when prayer has become impossible and your heart has turned to stone.

If you have never had any distractions you don't know how to pray. For the secret of prayer is a hunger for God and for the vision of God, a hunger that lies far deeper than the level of language or affection. And a man whose memory and imagination are persecuting him with a crowd of useless or even evil thoughts and images may sometimes be forced to pray far better, in the depths of his murdered heart, than one whose mind is swimming with clear concepts and brilliant purposes and easy acts of love.

*O*ur minds are like crows. They pick up everything that glitters, no matter how uncomfortable our nests get with all that metal in them.

I wonder if there are twenty men alive in the world now, who see things as they really are. That would mean that there were twenty men who were free, who were not dominated or even influenced by any attachment to any created thing or to their own selves or to any gift of God, even to the highest, the most supernaturally pure of His graces. I don't believe that there are twenty such men alive in the world. But there must be one or two. They are the ones who are holding everything together and keeping the universe from falling apart.

The whole problem of our time is the problem of love: how are we going to recover the ability to love ourselves and to love one another? The reason why we hate one another and fear one another is that we secretly or openly hate and fear our own selves. And we hate ourselves because the depths of our being are a chaos of frustration and spiritual misery. Lonely and helpless, we cannot be at peace with others because we are not at peace with ourselves, and we cannot be at peace with ourselves because we are not at peace with God.

The concept of "VIRTUE" does not appeal to men, because they are no longer interested in becoming good. Yet if you tell them that Saint Thomas talks about virtues as "habits of the practical intellect" they may, perhaps, pay some attention to your words. They are pleased with the thought of anything that would seem to make them clever.

I have very little idea of what is going on in the world: but occasionally I happen to see some of the things they are drawing and writing there and it gives me the conviction that they are all living in ash-cans. It makes me glad I cannot hear what they are singing.

*I*f a writer is so cautious that he never writes anything that cannot be criticized, he will never write anything that can be read. If you want to help other people you have got to make up your mind to write things that some men will condemn.

*P*erhaps I am stronger than I think.
Perhaps I am even afraid of my strength, and turn it against myself, thus making my-

self weak. Making myself secure. Making myself guilty.

Perhaps I am most afraid of the strength of God in me. Perhaps I would rather be guilty and weak in myself, than strong in Him whom I cannot understand.

The poet enters into himself in order to create. The contemplative enters into God in order to be created.

When humility delivers a man from attachment to his own works and his own reputation, he discovers that true joy is only possible when we have completely forgotten ourselves. And it is only when we pay no more attention to our own life and our own reputation and our own excellence that we are at last completely free to serve God in perfection for His own sake alone.

*A*t the root of all war is fear: not so much the fear men have of one another as the fear they have of *everything*. It is not merely that they do not trust one another: they do not even trust themselves. If they are not sure when someone else may turn around and kill them, they are still less sure when they may turn around and kill themselves. They cannot trust anything, because they have ceased to believe in God.

*O*n my forty-sixth birthday they put an ape into space. They shot him farther than they intended. They recovered him alive. He flew through space at a fabulous speed, pressing buttons, pulling levers, eating banana-flavored pills. He signaled with faultless regularity, just as he had been trained to do. He did not complain of space. He did not complain of time. He did not complain either of earth or heaven.

He was bothered by no metaphysical problems. He felt no guilt. At least it is not reported that he felt any guilt.

Why should an ape in space feel guilt? Space is where there is no more weight and no more guilt. And an ape does not feel guilt even on earth, for that matter.

Would that we on earth did not feel guilt! Perhaps if we can all get into space we will not feel any more guilt. We will pull levers, press buttons, eat banana-flavored pills. No, pardon me. We are not quite apes yet.

We will not feel guilt in space. We will not feel guilt on the moon. Maybe we will feel just a *little* guilt on the moon, but when we get to Mars we will feel no guilt at all.

From Mars or the moon we will blow up the world, perhaps. If we blow up the world from the moon we may feel a little guilt. If we blow it up from Mars we will feel no guilt at all. No guilt at all. We will blow up the world with no guilt at all. Tra la. Push the buttons, press the levers! As soon as they get a factory on Mars for banana-colored apes there will be no guilt at all.

I am forty-six years old. Let's be quite

serious. Civilization has deigned to grace my forty-sixth birthday with this marvelous feat, and I should get ribald about it? Let me learn from this contented ape. He pressed buttons. He pulled levers. They shot him too far. Never mind. They fished him out of the Atlantic and he shook hands with the Navy.

*W*ill you end wars by asking men to trust men who evidently cannot be trusted? No. Teach them to love and trust God; then they will be able to love the men they cannot trust, and will dare to make peace with them, not trusting in them but in God.

For only love—which means humility— can cast out the fear which is the root of all war.

*P*erhaps peace is not, after all, something you work for, or "fight for." It is indeed "fighting for peace" that starts all the wars. What, after all, are the pretexts of all these Cold War crises, but "fighting for peace?" Peace is something you have or you do not have. If you are yourself at peace, then there is at least *some* peace in the world. Then share your peace with everyone, and everyone will be at peace. Of course I realize that arguments like this can be used as a pretext for passivity, for indifferent acceptance of every iniquity. Quietism leads to war as surely as anything does. But I am not speaking of quietism, because quietism is not peace, nor is it the way to peace.

*I*f men really wanted peace they would ask God and He would give it to them. But why should He give the world a peace which it does not really desire? For the peace the world seems to desire is really no peace at all.

To some men peace merely means the liberty to exploit other people without fear of retaliation or interference. To others peace means the freedom to rob one another without interruption. To still others it means the leisure to devour the goods of the earth without being compelled to interrupt their pleasures to feed those whom their greed is starving. And to practically everybody peace simply means the absence of any physical violence that might cast a shadow over lives devoted to the satisfaction of their animal appetites for comfort and pleasure.

Many men like these have asked God for what they thought was "peace" and wondered why their prayer was not answered. They could not understand that it actually *was* answered. God left them with what they desired, for their idea of peace was only another form of war.

So instead of loving what you think is peace, love other men and love God above all. And instead of hating the people you think are warmakers, hate the appetites and the disorder in your own soul, which are the causes of war.

*I*t is only the infinite mercy and love of God that has prevented us from tearing ourselves to pieces and destroying His entire creation long ago. People seem to think that it is in some way a proof that no merciful God exists, if we have so many wars. On the contrary, consider how in spite of centuries of sin and greed and lust and cruelty and hatred and avarice and oppression and injustice, spawned and bred by the free wills of men, the human race can still recover, each time, and can still produce men and women who overcome evil with good, hatred with love, greed with charity, lust and cruelty with sanctity. How could all this be possible without the merciful love of God, pouring out His grace upon us? Can there be any doubt where wars come from and where peace comes from, when the children of this world, excluding God from their peace conferences, only manage to bring about greater and greater wars the more they talk about peace?

*I*t is principally in the suffering and sacrifice that are demanded for men to live together in peace and harmony that love is perfected in us, that we are prepared for contemplation.

A letter arrives stamped with the slogan "The U.S. Army, key to peace." No army is the key to peace, neither the U.S. Army nor the Soviet Army nor any other. No "great" nation has the key to anything but war.

Power has nothing to do with peace. The more men build up military power, the more they violate peace and destroy it.

*F*rom moment to moment I remember with astonishment that I am at the same time empty and full, and satisfied because I am empty. I lack nothing. The Lord rules me.

*Y*esterday I killed a big, shiny, black widow spider in her nest in a rotten tree stump. A beautiful spider, more beautiful than most other kinds. But I thought I had better kill her, for I myself had sat down right next to the stump before I saw her there. Someone else might do the same and get bitten.

It is strange to be so very close to something that can kill you, and not be defended by some kind of an invention. As if, wherever there was a problem in life, some machine would have to get there before you to negotiate it. As if we could not deal with the serious things of life except through the intermediary of these angels, our inventions.

As if life were nothing, death were nothing. As if the whole of reality were in the inventions that stand between us and the world: the inventions which have become our world.

*F*ree will is not given to us merely as a firework to be shot off into the air. There are some men who seem to think their acts are freer in proportion as they are without purpose, as if a rational purpose imposed some kind of limitation upon us. That is like saying that one is richer if he throws money out the window than if he spends it.

Since money is what it is, I do not deny that you may be worthy of all praise if you light your cigarettes with it. That would show you had a deep, pure sense of the ontological value of the dollar. Nevertheless, if that is all you can think of doing with money you will not long enjoy the advantages that it can still obtain.

It may be true that a rich man can better afford to throw money out the window than a poor man, but neither the spending nor the waste of money is what makes a man rich. He is rich by virtue of what he has, and his riches are valuable to him for what he can do with them.

As for freedom, according to this analogy, it grows no greater by being wasted, or spent, but it is given to us as a talent to be traded with until the coming of Christ. In this trading we part with what is ours only to recover it with interest. We do not destroy it or throw it away. We dedicate it to some purpose, and this dedication makes us freer than we were before.

*A*fter the great Chilean earthquake, after bigger and bigger bombs, after a plague of sharks along the California beaches, it is finally reported that near San Francisco a whale was washed ashore dead—of ulcers!

*W*e are so convinced that past evils must repeat themselves that we make them repeat themselves. We dare not risk a new life in which the evils of the past are totally forgotten; a new life seems to imply new evils, and we would rather face evils that are already familiar. Hence we cling to the evil that has already become ours, and renew it from day to day, until we become identified with it and change is no longer thinkable.

*I*t is easy enough to tell the poor to accept their poverty as God's will when you yourself have warm clothes and plenty of food and medical care and a roof over your head and no worry about the rent. But if you want them to believe you—try to share some of their poverty and see if you can accept it as God's will yourself!

Thomas Merton.

At Columbia, with Robert Lax.

At the hermitage.

The Abbey of Gethsemani.

With the Dalai Lama in 1968.

The hills are blue and hot. There is a brown, dusty field in the bottom of the valley. I hear a machine, a bird, a clock. The clouds are high and enormous. Through them the inevitable jet plane passes: this time probably full of passengers from Miami to Chicago. What passengers? This I have no need to decide. They are out of my world, up there, busy sitting in their small, isolated, arbitrary lounge that does not even seem to be moving—the lounge that somehow unaccountably picked them up off the earth in Florida to suspend them for a while with timeless cocktails and then let them down in Illinois. The suspension of modern life in contemplation that *gets you somewhere*!

There are also other worlds above me. Other jets will pass over, with other contemplations and other modalities of intentness.

I have seen the SAC plane, with the bomb in it, fly low over me and I have looked up out of the woods directly at the closed bay of the metal bird with a scientific egg in its breast! A womb easily and mechanically

47

opened! I do not consider this technological mother to be the friend of anything I believe in. However, like everyone else, I live in the shadow of the apocalyptic cherub. I am surveyed by it, impersonally. Its number recognizes my number. Are these numbers preparing at some moment to coincide in the benevolent mind of a computer? This does not concern me, for I live in the woods as a reminder that I am free not to be a number.

There is, in fact, a choice.

*I*n an age where there is much talk about "being yourself" I reserve to myself the right to forget about being myself, since in any case there is very little chance of my being anybody else. Rather it seems to me that when one is too intent on "being himself" he runs the risk of impersonating a shadow.

Yet I cannot pride myself on special freedom, simply because I am living in the woods. I am accused of living in the woods like Thoreau instead of living in the desert like St. John the Baptist. All I can answer is that I am not living "like anybody." Or "unlike anybody." We all live somehow or other, and that's that. It is a compelling necessity for me to be free to embrace the necessity of my own nature.

I exist under trees. I walk in the woods out of necessity. I am both a prisoner and an escaped prisoner. I cannot tell you why, born in France, my journey ended here in Kentucky. It makes no difference. Do I have a "day"? Do I spend my "day" in a "place"? I know there are trees here. I know there are birds here. I know the birds in fact very well, for there are precise pairs of birds (two each of fifteen or twenty species) living in the immediate area of my cabin. I share this particular place with them: we form an ecological balance. This harmony gives the idea of "place" a new configuration.

As to the crows, they form part of a different pattern. They are vociferous and self-justifying, like humans. They are not two, they are many. They fight each other and the other birds, in a constant state of war.

There is a mental ecology, too, a living balance of spirits in this corner of the woods. There is room here for many other songs besides those of birds. Of Vallejo for instance. Or Rilke, or René Char, Montale, Zukofsky, Ungaretti, Edwin Muir, Quasimodo or some Greeks. Or the dry, disconcerting voice of Nicanor Parra, the poet of the sneeze. Here is also Chuang Tzu whose climate is perhaps most the climate of this silent corner of woods. A climate in which there is no need for explanations. Here is the reassuring companionship of many silent Tzu's and Fu's; Kung Tzu, Lao Tzu, Meng Tzu, Tu Fu. And Hui Neng. And Chao-Chu. And the drawings of Sengai. And a big graceful scroll from Suzuki. Here also is a Syrian hermit called Philoxenus. An Algerian cenobite called Camus. Here is heard the clanging prose of Tertullian, with the dry catarrh of Sartre. Here the voluble dissonances of Auden, with the golden sounds of John of Salisbury. Here is the deep vegetation of that more ancient forest in which the angry birds, Isaias and Jeremias, sing. Here should be, and are, feminine voices from Angela of Foligno to Flannery O'Connor, Theresa of Avila, Juliana of Norwich, and, more personally and warmly still, Raissa Maritain. It is good to choose the voices that will be heard in these woods, but they also choose themselves, and send themselves here to be present in this silence. In any case there is no lack of voices.

*T*his is not a hermitage—it is a house. ("Who was that hermitage I seen you with last night? . . .") What I wear is pants. What I do is live. How I pray is breathe. Who said Zen? Wash out your mouth if you said Zen. If you see a meditation going by, shoot it. Who said "Love"? Love is in the movies. The spiritual life is something that people worry about when they are so busy with something else they think they ought to be spiritual. Spiritual life is guilt. Up here in the woods is seen the New Testament: that is to say, the wind comes through the trees and you breathe it. Is it supposed to be clear? I am not inviting anybody to try it. Or suggesting that one day the message will come saying Now. That is none of my business.

I am out of bed at two-fifteen in the morning, when the night is darkest and most silent. Perhaps this is due to some ailment or other. I find myself in the primordial lost-ness of night, solitude, forest, peace, a mind awake in the dark, looking for a light, not totally reconciled to being out of bed. A light appears, and in the light an ikon. There is now in the large darkness a small room of radiance with psalms in it. The psalms grow up silently by themselves without effort like plants in this light which is favorable to them. The plants hold themselves up on stems which have a single consistency, that of mercy, or rather great mercy. *Magna misericordia.* In the formlessness of night and silence a word then pronounces itself: Mercy. It is surrounded by other words of lesser consequence: " Destroy iniquity" "Wash me" " Purify" "I know my iniquity." *Peccavi.* Concepts without interest in the world of business, war, politics, culture, etc. Concepts also often without serious interest to ecclesiastics.

Other words: Blood. Guile. Anger. The way that is not good. The way of blood, guile, anger, war.

Out there the hills in the dark lie south-ward. The way over the hills is blood, guile, dark, anger, death: Selma, Birmingham, Mississippi. Nearer than these, the atomic city,* from which each day a freight car of fission-

*Oak Ridge, Tennessee.

able material is brought to be laid carefully beside the gold in the underground vault which is at the heart of this nation.

"Their mouth is the opening of the grave; their tongues are set in motion by lies; their heart is void."

Blood, lies, fire, hate, the opening of the grave, void. Mercy, great mercy.

The birds begin to wake. It will soon be dawn. In an hour or two the towns will wake, and men will enjoy everywhere the great luminous smiles of production and business.

*A*ll monks, as is well known, are unmarried, and hermits more unmarried than the rest of them. Not that I have anything against women. I see no reason why a man can't love God and a woman at the same time. If God was going to regard women with a jealous eye, why did he go and make them in the first place? There is a lot of talk about a married clergy. Interesting. So far there has not been a great deal said about married hermits. Well, anyway, I have the place full of ikons of the Holy Virgin.

One might say I had decided to marry the

silence of the forest. The sweet dark warmth of the whole world will have to be my wife. Out of the heart of that dark warmth comes the secret that is heard only in silence, but it is the root of all the secrets that are whispered by all the lovers in their beds all over the world. So perhaps I have an obligation to preserve the stillness, the silence, the poverty, the virginal point of pure nothingness which is at the center of all other loves. I attempt to cultivate this plant without comment in the middle of the night and water it with psalms and prophecies in silence. It becomes the most rare of all the trees in the garden, at once the primordial paradise tree, the *axis mundi*, the cosmic axle, and the Cross. *Nulla silva talem profert.* There is only one such tree. It cannot be multiplied. It is not interesting.

—Why live in the woods?
—Well, you have to live somewhere.
—Do you get lonely?
—Yes, sometimes.
—Are you mad at people?
—No.
—Are you mad at the monastery?
—No.

—What do you think about the future of
  monasticism?
—Nothing. I don't think about it.
—Is it true that your bad back is due to Yoga?
—No.
—Is it true that you are practising Zen in
  secret?
—Pardon me, I don't speak English.

*I*t is necessary for me to see the first point of
light which begins to be dawn. It is necessary
to be present alone at the resurrection of Day,
in the blank silence when the sun appears. In
this completely neutral instant I receive from
the Eastern woods, the tall oaks, the one
word "DAY," which is never the same. It is
never spoken in any known language.

*R*ituals. Washing out the coffee pot in the
rain bucket. Approaching the outhouse with
circumspection on account of the king snake
who likes to curl up on one of the beams
inside. Addressing the possible king snake
in the outhouse and informing him that he

should not be there. Asking the formal ritual question that is asked at this time every morning: "Are you in there?"

*M*ore rituals: Spray bedroom (cockroaches and mosquitoes). Close all the windows on south side (heat). Leave windows open on north and east sides (cool). Leave windows open on west side until maybe June when it gets very hot on all sides. Pull down shades. Get water bottle. Rosary. Watch. Library book to be returned.

It is time to visit the human race.

I start out under the pines. The valley is already hot. Machines out there in the bottoms, perhaps planting corn. Fragrance of the woods. Cool west wind under the oaks. Here is the place on the path where I killed a copperhead. There is the place where I saw the fox run daintily and carefully for cover carrying a rabbit in his mouth. And there is the cement cross that, for no reason, the novices rescued from the corner of a destroyed wall and put up in the woods: people imagine someone is buried there. It is just a cross. Why should there not be a cement cross by itself in the middle of the woods?

A squirrel is kidding around somewhere overhead in midair. Tree to tree. The coquetry of flight.

I come out into the open over the hot hollow and the old sheep barn. Over there is the monastery, bugging with windows, humming with action.

The long yellow side of the monastery faces the sun on a sharp rise with fruit trees and beehives. This is without question one of the least interesting buildings on the face of the earth. However, in spite of the most earnest efforts to deprive it of all character and keep it ugly, it is surpassed in this respect by the vast majority of other monasteries. It is so completely plain that it ends, in spite of itself, by being at least simple. A lamentable failure of religious architecture—to come so close to non-entity and yet not fully succeed! I climb sweating into the novitiate, and put down my water bottle on the cement floor. The bell is ringing. I have duties, obligations, since here I am a monk. When I have accomplished these, I return to the woods where I am nobody. In the choir are the young monks, patient, serene, with very clear eyes, thin, reflective, gentle, confused. Today perhaps I tell them of Eliot's *Little Gidding*, analyzing the first movement of the poem ("Midwinter spring is its own season"). They will listen with attention thinking some other person is talking to them about some other poem.

*I*n the heat of noon I return with the water bottle freshly filled, through the cornfield, past the barn under the oaks, up the hill, under the pines, to the hot cabin. Larks rise out of the long grass singing. A bumblebee hums under the wide shady eaves.

I sit in the cool back room, where words cease to resound, where all meanings are absorbed in the *consonantia* of heat, fragrant pine, quiet wind, bird song and one central tonic note that is unheard and unmuttered. This is no longer a time of obligations. In the silence of the afternoon all is present and all is inscrutable in one central tonic note to which every other sound ascends or descends, to which every other meaning aspires, in order to find its true fulfillment. To ask when the note will sound is to lose the afternoon: it has already sounded, and all things now hum with the resonance of its sounding.

*C*hanting the *alleluia* in the second mode: strength and solidity of the Latin, seriousness of the second mode, built on the *re* as though on a sacrament, a presence. One keeps returning to the *re* as to an inevitable presence. One keeps returning to the *re* as to an inevitable center. *Sol-Re, Fa-Re, Sol-Re, Do-Re.* Many other notes in between, but suddenly one hears only the one note. *Consonantia:* all notes, in their perfect distinctness, are yet blended in one. (Through a curious oversight Gregorian chant has continued to be sung in this monastery. But not for long.)

*I*n the refectory is read a message of the Pope, denouncing war, denouncing the bombing of civilians, reprisals on civilians, killing of hostages, torturing of prisoners (all in Vietnam). Do the people of this country realize who the Pope is talking about? They have by now become so solidly convinced that the Pope never denounces anybody but Communists that they have long since ceased to listen. The monks seem to know. The voice of the reader trembles.

I sweep. I spread a blanket out in the sun. I cut grass behind the cabin. I write in the heat of the afternoon. Soon I will bring the blanket in again and make the bed. The sun is over-clouded. The day declines. Perhaps there will be rain. A bell rings in the monastery. A devout Cistercian tractor growls in the valley. Soon I will cut bread, eat supper, say psalms, sit in the back room as the sun sets, as the birds sing outside the window, as night descends on the valley. I become surrounded once again by all the silent Tzu's and Fu's (men without office and without obligation). The birds draw closer to their nests. I sit on the cool straw mat on the floor, considering the bed in which I will presently sleep alone under the ikon of the Nativity.

Meanwhile the metal cherub of the apocalypse passes over me in the clouds, treasuring its egg and its message.

The selections in this book were taken from the following works of Thomas Merton: *Selected Poems, Seeds of Contemplation, New Seeds of Contemplation*, New Directions; *Conjectures of a Guilty Bystander*, Doubleday; *The Seven Storey Mountain, The Sign of Jonas, No Man Is an Island*, Harcourt, Brace & World; *The Living Bread*, Farrar, Straus & Cudahy. "Day of a Stranger" originally appeared in *The Hudson Review*.

The next morning at breakfast she found Emily sipping tea and William practising turning the colour of his hot buttered toast. Today was the day that preparations for the fete began in earnest, and the house was a hive of activity.

Ada was excited too, but she couldn't shake the feeling that something strange was going on; she was worried about Marylebone, and it was her birthday in two days, which everyone had most likely forgotten again. It had put her in rather a funny mood.

'Don't play with your food, William,' said Emily, putting down her teacup and taking a bite of a chocolate eclair in the shape of the Prince Regent.

'Cake for breakfast?' said Ada.

'There's plenty to choose from,' said Emily, pointing at the Jacobean sideboard. 'I think the cooks have been practising.'

Ada gasped. Emily was right. Piled high on the sideboard was a magnificent display of baked goods.

There was a pile of rocky-looking macaroons glued together with lemon curd from the Hairy Hikers. Next to that were Nigellina Sugarspoon's giant chocolate sponge in a lake of melted chocolate and Gordon Ramsgate's eye-wateringly fiery croissants. Mary Huckleberry had baked half a dozen tiny but perfectly formed cakes, but Ada's eye was drawn to the creation at the end. A beautifully sculpted princess made of toasted brioche sat on a cushion of fluffy scrambled egg

A CAIRN OF CUMBRIAN MACAROONS

CHOCOLATE FINGER-LICKING UPSIDE DOWN CAKE

EXTREMELY CROSS CROISSANTS WITH CHILLI PEPPER DUSTING

BABY VICTORIA SPONGES WITH AN AMUSEMENT OF PLUM JAM

from which, like the rays of the sun, came cheesy sponge fingers. A little card beside it said:

Shall I compare Thee to A Summer's Trifle

BREAKFAST BRIOCHE WITH STILTON SOLAR FLARES

Compliments of HESTON HARBOIL

The plate next to it contained a small baby rusk and a rather messy bacon roll.

'They're William Flake's Pastries of Innocence and

INNOCENCE AND EXPERIENCE

THE PRINCE REGENT AS AN ECLAIR

Experience,' said Emily doubtfully. 'I prefer this eclair made by Hollyhead – the chocolate trousers are delicious!'

Ada helped herself to a little of Heston Harboil's brioche and egg, which tasted as good as it looked. Just then, there was the sound of carriage wheels on gravel and Emily jumped up from her seat and rushed over to the window.

'They're here! They're here!' she exclaimed excitedly. 'The painters are here!'

Ada and William joined Emily at the window.

A stagecoach had drawn up in front of the steps, and a group of rather strange-looking men were attempting to climb out of it. They all carried easels, paintboxes, bundles of paintbrushes and canvases which kept getting wedged in the windows, or being dropped on the ground as the occupants of the stagecoach squeezed through the door.

The stagecoach itself was rather battered, but brightly painted and pulled by four extremely large carthorses with brass nameplates on their bridles which read 'Titian', 'Rembrandt', 'Damian' and 'Tracey'. On the side of the stagecoach in decorative lettering was written 'Beauty for the Price of a Raffle Ticket'.

'Real live painters!' breathed Emily, grabbing her watercolour box and her portfolio. 'Come on, Ada, let's go and meet them!'

Ada had never seen Emily quite this excited, not even when they'd discovered the purple geranium of Cairo growing behind the old icehouse.

Emily grasped her by the hand and led Ada down the stairs, across the hall, out through the front door and to the top of the steps outside. All the painters had managed to get out of the stagecoach, although one, an enormous man with a bushy beard, was having difficulty getting down from his seat on the roof because his wooden clogs wouldn't fit on the rungs of the ladder attached to the side.

They lined up at the foot of the steps, and their leader, a short man in an extremely tall hat and with a rather intense expression on his face, cleared his throat.

'We are the finest painters in England!' he announced. 'Our paintings have been reproduced on chocolate boxes and cake tins throughout the land, but we do not believe in selling our pictures to the highest bidder.'

He smiled and produced a roll of numbered tickets from his waistcoat. 'Instead the humblest art lover has the chance to win a pretty picture for a single penny!'

'What a lovely idea!' said Emily.

'My dear young ladies,' said the painter, raising his extremely tall hat, 'the Brotherhood of Twee Raffelites at your service. I am J.M.W. Turnip, and these are my colleagues, Romney Marsh, Maxim de Trumpet-Oil, Stubby George and . . .' There was a loud thump and the crunch

J.M.W. TURNIP

ROMNEY MARSH

MAXIM DE TRUMPET-OIL

of pebbles as the enormous man with the bushy beard fell off the stagecoach roof. '*And* our very dear friend, Sir Stephen Belljar the clog-dancing cartoonist.'

Sir Stephen Belljar climbed to his feet and the crunching of pebbles grew louder as he did a shuffling, stomping dance.

'He's far too modest to tell you,' said J.M.W. Turnip, 'but Sir Stephen's famous for his caricature of the Prince Regent as a Cumberland sausage.'

'Gentlemen,' said a dry voice and, turning round, Ada saw that Maltravers had crept up and was standing behind her, 'rooms have been prepared for you all in the east wing. I'll send the grooms to bring up your luggage.'

Just then the sun disappeared behind dark clouds and Ada heard the distant rumble of thunder.

'Is that a watercolour box on your back?' J.M.W. Turnip asked Emily.

'Yes,' said Emily, smiling delightedly.

'Excellent!' said J.M.W. Turnip, clapping his hands together, before glancing up at the sky.

'Then take me to the tallest tree in the grounds –
we've no time to lose!'

OLD HARDY

Chapter Seven

J.M.W. Turnip followed Emily down
the steps and out across the dear-deer
park, where the herd of extremely expensive
ornamental deer were quietly grazing, along with
Lord Goth's collection of oblong sheep and
rectangular cattle.

'Where's Emily going?' Arthur Halford asked
Ada. He and the other grooms had just arrived
from the hobby-horse stables.

'Never mind about that, Halford,' wheezed
Maltravers. 'Unload that luggage and take it up
to the third floor of the east wing, and look lively
about it!'

Arthur and the grooms set to work. There were
trunks, easels and portfolios piled high inside the
stagecoach and four carpet bags belonging to Sir
Stephen Belljar strapped to the roof.

'See you tonight at the Attic Club,' Arthur whispered to Ada, before following the other grooms inside.

BATHSHEBA

TESS

FANCYDAY

THE FOUR GABRIELS

GABRIEL BEECH ON THE HIGGLEDY-PIGGLEDY

THE AMBRIDGE SISTERS

GABRIEL ACORN ON THE SAGBUTT

THE GORMLESS QUIRE

Ada set off across the dear-deer park as dark storm clouds gathered overhead. She knew exactly where Emily was going. She was taking J.M.W. Turnip

GABRIEL CHESTNUT
ON THE
CUMBRIAN SERPENT

to the tallest tree in the grounds, 'Old Hardy', an ancient greenwood tree in the middle of the park with a band-stand beneath it where the Gormless Quire, a village band, played unlikely instruments at random times of the day and night.

GABRIEL SYCAMORE
ON THE
GRUFFLEHORN

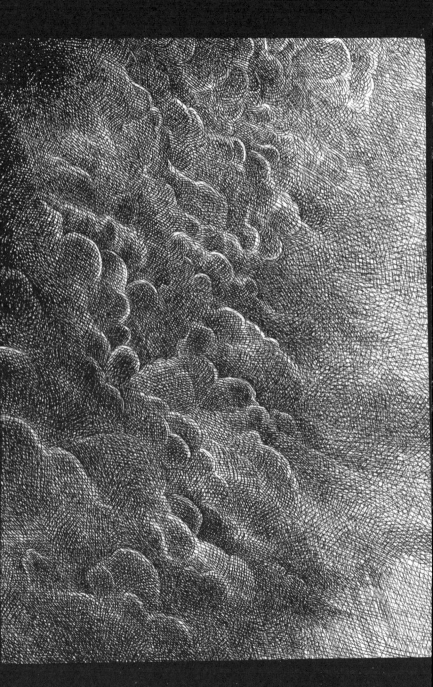

Sure enough, as Ada approached the tree, she saw Emily and J.M.W. Turnip standing under it.

The painter had taken off his jacket and extremely tall hat, given them to Emily to hold and strapped her watercolour box to his back. He turned to the tree and began climbing its knobbly trunk. Ada saw that he had a notebook clamped between his teeth as he used both arms to grasp branches and pull himself up.

'This is so exciting,' said Emily, 'watching a real painter at work! Mr Turnip is a painter of storms and sunsets, Ada. He says there are no heights an artist shouldn't climb to get the best view!'

Ada and Emily looked up. J.M.W. Turnip was being true to his word. He was almost at the top of the greenwood tree, on a thin, swaying branch. The wind grew stronger and thunder rumbled. As they watched, he unbuckled his belt and used it to strap himself securely to the branch. Then he took a pencil from behind his ear, the notebook from his mouth, opened it and . . .

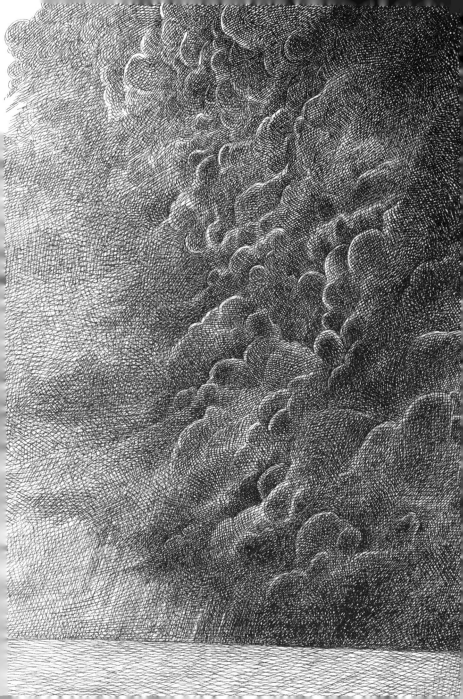

The clouds parted and bright sunshine bathed Ghastly-Gorm Hall and the dear-deer park. As quickly as they had gathered, the storm clouds drifted away and were replaced by a clear blue sky.

Strapped to the highest branch of 'Old Hardy', J.M.W. Turnip looked utterly dejected.

'Is it too much to ask for the odd summer storm?' he complained, shaking a fist at the sky. 'A tempest or two? The occasional maelstrom? Treetops, church steeples, the masts of sailing ships! I've strapped myself to them all,' he moaned. 'And every time! Every time –' he snapped his notebook shut – '*this* happens!' J.M.W. Turnip shielded his eyes as he stared at the sun.

'I'll just have to settle for the sunsets . . .' he

muttered, as he untied himself and began to climb down the tree. 'If only they weren't so picturesque.'

Ada and Emily waited patiently under the greenwood tree until J.M.W. Turnip reached the bottom. Emily handed him his jacket and hat and he gave Emily her watercolours back.

'Are you all right, Mr Turnip?' asked Emily.

'Oh . . . er . . . yes, my dear,' he replied, pulling on his jacket and putting his hat on his head. 'I just wish sometimes that my paintings weren't quite so pretty.'

'I would love to see them,' said Emily.

'You shall, my dear,' said J.M.W. Turnip, his face brightening. 'At our exhibition and raffle at the Full-Moon Fete . . . Talking of which,' he said, gazing across the park at the gravel drive, 'here the Spiegel tent comes now, in that Cumbrian juggernaut.'

Coming through the gates and rumbling up the drive was the biggest cart Ada had ever seen. It was pulled by a team of eight hairy oxen* and driven by a lady in a stovepipe bonnet and dark glasses.

Ada, Emily and J.M.W. Turnip walked back towards the house.

Maltravers appeared at the top of the steps. The Cumbrian juggernaut came to a halt in front of Ghastly-Gorm Hall.

'Spiegel tent,' said the lady in the stovepipe bonnet. 'Where do you want it?'

'Round the back,' Maltravers told her.

*Hairy oxen are very bad-tempered, particularly when having their coats brushed. They are also very smelly and produce sour-tasting milk. Also known as yucky yaks.

'The chimney caretaker will show you the way.'

Ada saw Kingsley coming towards the front of the house from the direction of the hobby-horse stables. The grooms trooped back out through the front door and joined him.

Somewhere from the depths of Ghastly-Gorm Hall, there came a long mournful whine.

'I've got other matters to attend to, so Kingsley's in charge,' Maltravers told the grooms. He turned and hurried back inside, slamming the door behind him.

The Cumbrian juggernaut lurched back into motion, as Kingsley, Arthur and the grooms walked ahead of the hairy oxen in the direction of the drawing-room garden.

'Well, since it's such a beautiful day, I think I'll have to make do with some landscape sketches,' said J.M.W. Turnip, without much enthusiasm.

'Can I sketch with you?' asked Emily,

her eyes wide with excitement.

'I'd be delighted,' replied J.M.W. Turnip, cheering up. 'There's a rather interesting feature over there,' he said, pointing to the Hill of Ambition, 'which will afford us excellent views.'

'But what about repotting the purple geranium?' Ada asked Emily.

'We can do that another time, Ada,' said Emily, hurrying after J.M.W. Turnip, who was striding off towards the hobby-horse racecourse.

Ada watched her go, feeling left out. Then she turned on her heels and walked along the gravel drive, following the deep grooves left by the wheels of the Cumbrian juggernaut. When she reached the drawing-room garden she found it in turmoil. The garden furniture had been cleared away and the hobby-horse grooms were running backwards and forwards across the lawn as they unloaded pieces of the Spiegel tent from the juggernaut, and tried not to trip up or get in each other's way.

'You break any of those and its seven years' bad luck,' shouted the driver of the juggernaut at a line of grooms struggling with large mirrors in decorative frames.

'And don't pet the oxen!' she called over. 'It only encourages them!'

The team of oxen stood in harness, ignoring the commotion around them as, shaggy heads down, they munched at the lawn.

Kingsley opened the book of instructions and started to read.

'Can I help?' asked Ada.

'Perhaps another time, Ada,' said Kingsley distractedly. He scratched his head as he turned the pages. 'If guy-rope D goes there, where does guy-rope E go? . . . oh, I see . . . then doll-rope two needs two pegs . . .'

Around them, the grooms hurried back and forth.

'Careful!' Ada turned round. It was Arthur Halford, in the middle of the lawn surrounded by bundles of rope and piles of tent pegs. 'Guys and dolls,' he called to the other grooms. 'Try not to get them mixed up. Round pegs to the left; square pegs to the right!' Ada stepped around the tent poles, decorative mirrors and brightly coloured canvas that were rapidly filling the lawn, until she reached Arthur.

'Is there anything I can do?' she asked.

Arthur smiled at her. 'That's fine, Ada,' he said cheerfully. 'We've got a system going. It's just like riding a hobby horse. Hold on tight and hope for the best!'

He hurried away to help the head groom, who'd just been butted in the stomach by a hairy ox.

Ada walked slowly away. In the bedroom garden, she bumped into William, who had taken his shirt off and was blending in beautifully with a bed of I-didn't-forget-yous.

'I don't suppose . . .' Ada began.

'Sorry, Ada,' said William, putting his shirt back on,

'but I'm late for my calculating-machine lesson in the Chinese drawing room. I was on my way there when I saw these,' he said, looking at the purple-and-yellow flowers, 'and I couldn't resist! I'll see you at the Attic Club tonight!' he called as he ran down the garden path and disappeared around the corner.

Ada went into the kitchen garden, where she found William Flake the baking poet and Ruby the outer-pantry maid standing next to an iron stove on wheels. 'It's very exciting,' said Ruby when she saw Ada. 'I'm helping Mr Flake bake his famous Jerusalem cake. It's a recipe from ancient times . . .'

CHARIOT
OF
FIRE

William Flake opened the stove door and peered inside before closing it again.

'It's rising nicely, Tyger-Tyger,' he chuckled, stroking his ginger cat as she brushed against his leg. 'Now for the icing . . .'

He straightened up and turned to Ruby.

'Ah, Ruby,' he beamed. 'Bring me my bowl of burning gold, bring me my spatulas of desire, bring me my whisk, and logs untold,' he chuckled, turning back to the stove with its gently smoking funnel, 'to fuel my chariot of fire!'

'Sorry, Ada,' said Ruby happily, 'I've got to dash. I don't want to keep Mr Flake waiting.'

She turned and ran into the kitchen.

Everybody was so busy, Ada thought miserably, as she walked away. Cooking, calculating, constructing . . . 'Everybody but me,' she sighed.

Chapter Eight

or the rest of the day, Ada kept herself busy. She went over to the hobby-horse stables and took out the smallest hobby horse she could find. It was called Tiny Timothy and was a bit rusty and rattly, but Ada's feet could just about touch the ground. Outside the stable door she saw one of the Twee Raffelites, Stubby

George, painting a portrait of Lord Goth's newest bicycle, the Lincoln Green Armchair. Sir Stephen Belljar was holding the hobby horse by the handlebars for him and shaking his head.

'A little too fancy for my tastes,' he muttered through his enormous bushy beard. 'Simple plank of wood between two cartwheels should be enough for any man.'

Ada rode over the cobbles and out across the west lawn, past the Alpine Gnome Rockery. Another of the Twee Raffelites, Maxim de Trumpet-Oil, had set up his easel and was painting a portrait of one of the gnomes.

It was life-size, and so real-looking that Ada felt she could almost reach into the picture and pick it up.

When she got to the hobby-horse racecourse she saw Emily and J.M.W. Turnip sketching on top of the Hill of Ambition. Ada waved but they were so engrossed in conversation that they didn't notice her.

THE HILLOCK
OF HUBRIS

THE HILL OF
AMBITION

Ada rode through the dear-deer park, the tiny animals scattering at her approach. Romney Marsh was sitting on the bandstand under 'Old Hardy', painting the portrait of an oblong sheep as it grazed nearby. Not wanting to disturb them, Ada steered a wide course around the overly ornamental fountain and back behind the new icehouse and then up towards the Lake of Extremely Coy Carp. By the time she got there, she

was quite hot. She climbed off the hobby horse and sat beside the lake in the sunshine. It was beautiful and had been the site of water meadows back in Anglo-Saxon times.

The Sensible Folly, a well-maintained copy of a Greek temple, where Maltravers lived, was reflected in the lake's still waters. There was no sign of the outdoor butler. Ada lay back and stared at the fluffy white clouds in the clear blue sky. What was he up to? she wondered sleepily. She should tell Lord Sydney about the strange grocers and their poodles, and ask him for the latest news on her father, and then there was Marylebone . . .

When Ada awoke, a bright full moon was reflected in the mirror-like surface of the lake. Ada sat up and stretched. 'I must have slept away the entire afternoon,' she said to herself, getting to her feet and climbing on to her hobby horse, 'Mind you, I have had some rather late nights recently . . .'

She rode back towards the house, and as she
approached the east gardens she gasped. There
in the centre of the drawing-room garden stood

the Spiegel tent. Kingsley, Arthur and the grooms had done a fine job. The tent looked magnificent in the moonlight.

Ada went up to the Spiegel tent's entrance,* which on closer inspection resembled a wardrobe. She pushed open the double doors and stepped inside.

The interior of the Spiegel tent was huge, with mirrors in ornate frames lining the circular walls in which Ada saw herself reflected back a hundred times.

'You dance beautifully,' said a voice from above, 'so wonderfully light on your feet.'

'And you are a most elegant partner . . .' came the reply in a light, lilting voice with just the trace of an accent.

Ada looked up. There, floating in mid-air, was her governess, Lucy Borgia, arm in arm with Lord Sydney Whimsy.

They were twirling slowly round and round, Lucy supporting Lord Whimsy by the waist and

Webbed Foot Notes

*The entrance to the Spiegel tent was made by Mr Tumnus, the cabinet-making faun, and his apprentice, Lucy.

131

arm. His pale blue eyes never left her face. In the mirrors surrounding them, Ada could see Lord Whimsy's reflection but not Lucy's. Ada gave an embarrassed little cough.

Lucy and Lord Sydney looked down.

'We have company, Lucy, my dear,' he said smoothly.

They floated to the ground and Lord Sydney stepped back and took a bow.

'You charming ladies will have to excuse me,' he said. 'In my line of work one's time is not one's own.'

He brushed past Ada and left the tent before she had a chance to ask him anything about Maltravers. Ada turned to her governess.

'Everybody is so busy with the Full-Moon Fete,' she complained, 'and I want to help Marylebone but she won't leave the wardrobe and Maltravers is up to something I'm sure of it and . . .'

Lucy reached out and took Ada's hand. Her touch was ice cold. 'I've been speaking to Lord Sydney,' she said, her eyes sparkling, 'and I've been telling him what a gifted pupil you are, Ada. He was very impressed by my reports of your umbrella fencing.'

'He was?' said Ada, pleased.

'Oh yes,' said Lucy. 'I'm sorry I've missed our lessons, but I've been helping Lord Sydney with his preparations for the fete . . .' She glanced at one of the mirrors that lined the wall. 'You know, Ada, I haven't seen my reflection in three hundred years . . .'

Ada could hear the sadness in her voice. 'I had my portrait

painted once by the young painter Lord Sydney so reminds me of. He said it was his masterpiece. I don't know what became of it. How I would love to see that picture again.' Ada saw Lucy's eyes fill with tears. 'Lord Sydney is a good man, a fine man . . . If only things were different . . .'

The governess turned away. 'Forgive me, Ada, but I feel quite unable to concentrate on lessons tonight.'

Lucy rose into the air, her arms raised, before transforming herself into a black bat and flapping

up towards the dome of the Spiegel tent. She flew around the hanging mirrorball, once, twice, before swooping out of one of the openings and disappearing into the night. Even Lucy was too distracted to spend time with her, Ada thought sadly.

Ada's tummy rumbled. She hadn't eaten since breakfast, she realized, and her supper would be waiting for her in her bedroom. She hoped it was something cooked by Heston Harboil.

After that there was the Attic Club meeting to go to. There would be plenty to talk about.

Ada caught her reflection in one of the mirrors. She hated to see Lucy Borgia so upset.

Then Ada smiled back at herself. Supper could wait; there was something she had to do first . . .

Chapter Nine

oud and shrill, like the sound of a seagull having its tail feathers plucked, the steam whistle sounded. Ada, who'd just stepped out of the Spiegel tent, stood rooted to the spot. Coming round the corner of the new icehouse was an enormous traction engine, with a tall black funnel belching out smoke, a round boiler and four huge iron wheels powered by steam. Behind it, the engine was pulling four black carriages with shuttered windows and pointy roofs.

The steam whistle toot-tooted again as the traction engine trundled through the gate of the drawing-room garden and came to a halt beside the Spiegel tent.

'What a beautiful moonlit night,' said a gloomy voice. 'You must be the little Goth girl.'

He was bald, white-faced, with extremely large

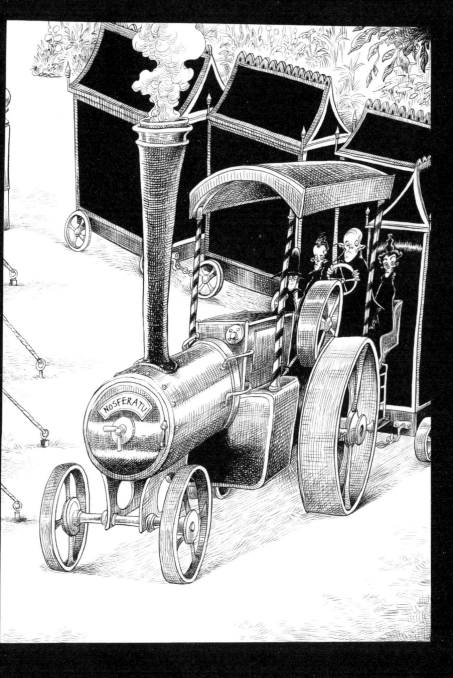

The Glum-Stokers

VLAD   GLAD   MLAD   BLAD

ears and, Ada saw, very long fingernails. He was
dressed all in black, and as he climbed down from
the traction engine he was followed by a white-
faced woman and two miserable-looking children.

'We're the Glum-Stokers,' said the driver with an expressive hand gesture. 'I'm Vlad and this is my wife Glad, and our children, Mlad and Blad.' He pointed a long bony finger at the traction engine and the carriages behind it.

'This is our Transylvanian Carnival,' he announced joylessly. 'All the fun of the fair . . .'

Ada followed the sweep of his curving fingernail and read the spiky white letters carefully painted on the pointy roofs of each carriage.

'Shy coconuts', 'Darren the Memory Goat', 'Bat Circus' and the one at the end which read 'Private – Keep Out'.

'That's where we sleep,' said Glad glumly.

The four of them exchanged looks, then turned back to Ada.

'No, please, don't bother,' said Vlad gloomily. 'We'll set everything up ourselves. With no help whatsoever. We always do. Don't let us keep you. If you see Lord Whimsy, can you tell him we're here?'

The four Glum-Stokers looked at Ada forlornly.

'I'll look forward to seeing your carnival,' said Ada politely. She climbed on to her hobby horse and set off awkwardly as the Glum-Stokers stared unblinkingly after her.

'Mirth and merriment,' said Glad stonily.

'Larks and laughter,' said Mlad and Blad, unsmiling.

'All the fun of the fair,' repeated Vlad soberly.

Once round the corner of the east wing, Ada broke into a run, the wheels of Tiny Timothy spinning over the gravel. She bypassed the west wing and raced over the cobbles towards the hobby-horse stables. What odd people to be running a carnival, she thought to herself.

But instead of stopping, Ada continued, past the unstable stables, with its sagging roof and walls propped up with scaffolding, and on towards the oldest part of Ghastly-Gorm Hall, the broken wing.*

Webbed Foot Notes

*The broken wing of Ghastly-Gorm Hall has many forgotten rooms containing interesting and obscure things such as ruby slippers, old fir trees and rolled-up carpets from Turkey.

It was called the broken wing because it was in need of repair. But it was out of sight at the back of the Hall, a jumble of rickety rooms, abandoned alcoves and crumbling chambers, and so was largely forgotten about.

Most of the rooms were empty but a few were filled with old, overlooked things – the sorts of things Ada liked best.

She stopped and propped Tiny Timothy against the wall, before opening a small arched door and entering. The broken wing had many winding, cobwebby corridors and could be confusing, but Ada and her friends in the Attic Club had been busy exploring.

They wrote about the discoveries they made, among other things, in their journal, *The Chimney Pot*.

Chimney Pot

Journal of the Attic Club

Dedicated to Exploring and Recording the Nooks, Crannies and Corners of Ghastly-Gorm Hall.

Nº1 Snow White and the Seven Dwarfs

A beautiful chimney of white stone and plaster this chimney leads down to the main kitchen of Ghastly-Gorm Hall and Mrs Beatem the Cook's oven, "Dante's Inferno." Note the chimney sweep escape door in Snow White's stack.

Nº4 The Lincoln Green Armchair

One of the most luxurious hobby horses, originally built in the Michigan Coachworks of the American Colonies by retired military man, General Motors. The finely upholstered armchair of green leather rests on an applewood frame with stylish "macaroni" handlebars.

Nº 5   A Porcelain Mozart "Big Nose" Gnome

Standing at the top of the rockery in the Gardens of Ghastly-Gorm Hall, this is a popular alpine gnome cast in distinctive pink porcelain from the famous garden ornament maker, Mozart of Salzburg. Unfortunately this gnome shows signs of blunderbuss damage.

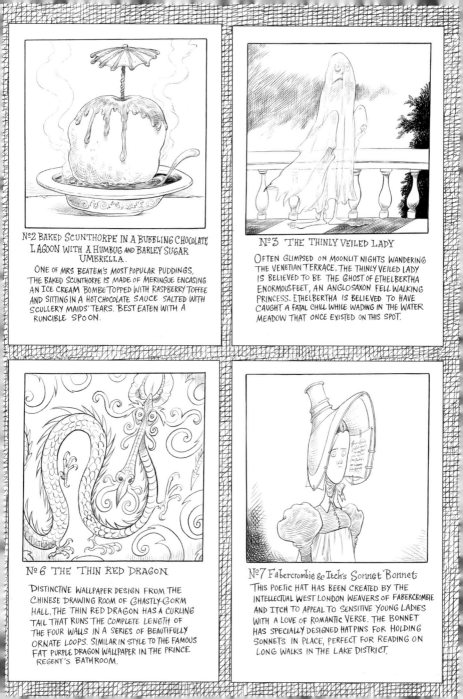

№2 BAKED SCUNTHORPE IN A BUBBLING CHOCOLATE LAGOON WITH A HUMBUG AND BARLEY SUGAR UMBRELLA.

ONE OF MRS BEATEM'S MOST POPULAR PUDDINGS, THE BAKED SCUNTHORPE IS MADE OF MERINGUE ENCASING AN ICE CREAM BOMBE TOPPED WITH RASPBERRY TOFFEE AND SITTING IN A HOT CHOCOLATE SAUCE SALTED WITH SCULLERY MAIDS' TEARS. BEST EATEN WITH A RUNCIBLE SPOON.

№3 THE THINLY VEILED LADY

OFTEN GLIMPSED ON MOONLIT NIGHTS WANDERING THE VENETIAN TERRACE, THE THINLY VEILED LADY IS BELIEVED TO BE THE GHOST OF ETHELBERTHA ENORMOUSFEET, AN ANGLOSAXON FELL WALKING PRINCESS. ETHELBERTHA IS BELIEVED TO HAVE CAUGHT A FATAL CHILL WHILE WADING IN THE WATER MEADOW THAT ONCE EXISTED ON THIS SPOT.

№6 THE THIN RED DRAGON

DISTINCTIVE WALLPAPER DESIGN FROM THE CHINESE DRAWING ROOM OF GHASTLY-GORM HALL, THE THIN RED DRAGON HAS A CURLING TAIL THAT RUNS THE COMPLETE LENGTH OF THE FOUR WALLS IN A SERIES OF BEAUTIFULLY ORNATE LOOPS. SIMILAR IN STYLE TO THE FAMOUS FAT PURPLE DRAGON WALLPAPER IN THE PRINCE REGENT'S BATHROOM.

№7 Fabercrombie & Itch's Sonnet Bonnet

THIS POETIC HAT HAS BEEN CREATED BY THE INTELLECTUAL WEST LONDON WEAVERS OF FABERCROMBIE AND ITCH TO APPEAL TO SENSITIVE YOUNG LADIES WITH A LOVE OF ROMANTIC VERSE. THE BONNET HAS SPECIALLY DESIGNED HATPINS FOR HOLDING SONNETS IN PLACE, PERFECT FOR READING ON LONG WALKS IN THE LAKE DISTRICT.

Ada knew exactly what she was looking for, and where to find it. She made her way quietly down several corridors, turning left, then right, until she came to a door she recognized. She opened it, and entered a long narrow room. A painting, wrapped in a sheet, was propped up against the far wall.

Ada went over and picked up the painting. Then she left the room and hurried down the cobwebby corridors without looking back. She'd tell her father about Maltravers taking in uninvited guests as soon as he got back from his book tour. But right now she was ready for her supper. She emerged from the broken wing into the entrance hall and climbed the stairs to her bedroom two at a time.

When she got there, she propped the painting against the mantelpiece and kicked off her shoes. Her supper was waiting for her on the more-than-occasional table. Ada lifted the lid and gave a little sigh.

It was one of Mrs Beat'em's cheese smellywiches (two slices of bread with a piece of Blue Gormly cheese between them). There was also a glass of milk and a generous slice of baked Scunthorpe for pudding.

It wasn't the Heston Harboil treat she'd been hoping for but Ada ate everything, even the humbug parasol stuck in the top of the baked Scunthorpe.

She was just about to go up to the top of the house for the Attic Club meeting when the door of the wardrobe in her dressing room opened, and the tip of a shiny black nose appeared.

Ada looked at the great-uncle clock on her mantelpiece. It was almost nine o'clock, the time the Attic Club began its weekly meeting.

But this was the first time her lady's maid had put so much as a nose outside of the wardrobe when Ada was in the room, and Ada didn't want to discourage her.

'Why don't you come out here?' said Ada. 'You can sit next to me on the Dalmatian divan and we can talk . . .'

The shiny black nose trembled and Ada heard a sad little sigh.

'There's only me here,' said Ada. 'There's nothing to be afraid of.'

There was a long pause. Ada sat down on the Dalmatian divan and pretended to examine her nails. Out of the corner of her eye, she saw Marylebone shuffle very slowly out of the wardrobe and pad across the Anatolian carpet. She had a red velvet cape with a fur-trimmed hood over one arm. Ada stared at a fingernail and waited.

The little bear reached the divan and sat shyly down. Ada glanced at Marylebone. Her lady's maid was wearing an apron with lots of pockets containing what looked like sewing needles and bundles of thread, and on the end of her nose a large pair of spectacles.

Ada reached over and squeezed Marylebone's paw. 'There's nothing to be afraid of,' she said. 'What happened to my mother was terrible,' she went on, 'and you have looked after me so well, Marylebone.'

Ada felt Marylebone's paw squeeze her hand.

'But,' said Ada, turning to Marylebone and looking straight into her rather startled eyes, 'now that my father and I are *so* much closer and I have my friends in the Attic Club, you could leave, Marylebone, and find happiness in Bolivia.'

Marylebone reached forward and put the red cape around Ada's shoulders.

Then she got up and padded over to the wardrobe and slipped inside.

Chapter Ten

da hurried up the stairs, to the very top of the grand staircase and then along the attic corridor that ran the length of the east wing. From behind the row of closed doors she heard the low, rumbling snores of the kitchen maids.

What with having supper, talking to her lady's maid and trying on her mother's cape and admiring it in the looking glass, Ada had quite lost track of the time.

The red cape reached almost to the floor, swishing around Ada's ankles. Its lined hood felt deliciously soft and warm, and when Ada pulled it up over her head and stared at her reflection, she felt wonderfully mysterious. But the best part of the cape was the carefully stitched label:

STITCHED WITH LOVE
FOR
Parthenope Goth
* CRUSHED VELVET *
ALPACA WOOL LINING

Ada reached the end of the corridor and turned the corner into a dark passageway. She stopped at the iron ladder fixed to the far wall and, swishing back her red cape, she climbed to the top and pushed open the trapdoor in the plaster ceiling.

She climbed through the opening into the huge attic beyond.

'Sorry I'm late,' she called. 'Have I missed anything?'

Ada stopped on the dusty floorboards and stared. The attic was empty. At its centre was a table made of fruit crates with six old coal sacks stuffed with dried haricot beans around it to sit on.

Ada walked over to the table. There was a copy of *The Chimney Pot – Journal of the Attic Club* on it, next to a wooden spoon, and on each of the bean sacks a handwritten note . . .

Dear Ada,

We've been putting up the Spiegel tent. Did you know 'Spiegel' is Dutch for mirror? Yours Sincerely

Arthur + K.

Dear Ada,

Sorry that we didn't wait but with the full Moon fete tomorrow night we've all been SO busy. I've been helping Mr Turnip organize the raffle!

love

Emily

Dear Ada,
   The Kitchens are
Very Very busy!
   William Flake
said my icing-sugar
footprint was the best
he'd seen on any
Jerusalem cake!
   Ruby x x

Dear Ada,
I've been
having calculating
lessons!
See you at
breakfast
William
Cabbage
Esq

Wearing her mother's cape had made Ada feel wonderful, but now she was feeling sad and lonely once again. She'd wanted to tell the Attic Club about the strange visitors that Maltravers had invited to Ghastly-Gorm Hall and ask their advice about how she could help Marylebone. But they were just as distracted by the Full-Moon Fete as everybody else.

Well, at least with the Full-Moon Fete tomorrow night, she could talk to her father. Lord Goth would be back from his book tour. Although he always looked rather bored, particularly during the pillow dancing, Lord Goth knew the villagers of Gormless expected him to be at the fete, and Ada knew he didn't like to disappoint them. She sat down on a bean sack and picked up the copy of *The Chimney Pot* . . .

Ada was the editor of the journal. She collected the accounts of interesting things each member had seen or found, and Emily did the drawings. Then Ada sent them on the Gormless mail coach* to be printed in London. When they came back, a copy was slid under every servant's door, and others were tied in a bundle and left on the bandstand for the villagers of Gormless to collect.

Ada and the other members of the Attic Club often overheard the mysterious journal being discussed but they never said anything because, as Emily Cabbage said firmly, 'What happens in the Attic Club stays in the Attic Club.'

Ada put down the journal and was just about to leave the attic when a dove flew through one of the small round windows that led out on to the rooftops.

It fluttered around the rafters before landing on the fruitcake table.

Ada took the note from its leg.

It is a far, far harder thing I ask, than I have ever asked...

I NEED YOUR HELP!

Meet me at the Spiegel tent.

Whimsy

So she hadn't been completely
forgotten after all!

Ada ran back down the attic
corridor
and jumped
on to the
banisters and
slid down from the attic,
past the murals of goddesses
chasing peeping huntsmen

and youths staring at
their reflections in pools.
She whooshed round
the bend and slid along

the third floor, the paintings of the passing by in a blur. Down from the third to the second floor Ada whizzed, past the Dutch paintings of kitchen tables crowded with groceries and washing-up. Round the corner and down to the first floor, then a last whooshing turn and the descent to the entrance hall, watched by the portraits of the previous Lords Goth, all five of them. Ada jumped to the marble floor and ran past the statues and out of the front door.

When she reached the Spiegel tent she was quite out of breath. Ada pushed open the double doors and looked inside. There was no sign of Lord Sydney.

'Roll up, roll up,' said a gloomy voice, and turning round Ada saw Vlad and the Glum-Stokers standing

THE 1ST LORD GOTH

THE 2ND LORD GOTH

THE 3RD LORD GOTH

THE 4TH LORD GOTH

THE 5TH LORD GOTH

behind her. Vlad waved an expressive hand at the carriages lined up beside the tent. Their sides were open, and their interiors lit by candles.

'We're ready for you,' said Glad with a sad smile.

'Ready for me?' said Ada.

'Step this way,' said Mlad and Blad glumly, taking her by the arm and guiding her over to the first carriage.

Three short-eared bats and a flying fox were hanging upside down above a small stage. As Ada watched, they flapped up into the air and began to fly in formation over her head. Then they swooped down to the stage, picked up hoops in their claws and flew back up into the night sky. The flying fox flew through each hoop in turn before performing a somersault. The bats returned to their perches.

'Well done, Basil. Good job, girls,' said Vlad unenthusiastically. Mlad and Blad guided Ada to the second carriage, where a row of mahogany cups stood in a row, each with a name carved into it.

'Nick, Nac, Sarawak, Giverdogger, Bone,' Ada read. Mlad handed her a toasting fork with a marshmallow on the end.

'Toast it on a candle,' said Blad gloomily.

Ada did as he suggested, holding the
marshmallow over one of the
candles that lit the stage.

THE
SHY COCONUTS

NICK   NAC   SARAWAK   GIVER DOGGER

A sweet smell rose into the air and, one after the other, a tiny shrunken head peered up over the lip of each mahogany cup.

'Now throw it,' said Mlad.

Ada tossed the marshmallow towards the cups and Giverdogger opened its mouth extra wide and caught the marshmallow in its teeth.

'More!' said Sarawak.

'More! More! More!' said Nick, Nac and Bone.

'Settle down, boys,' said Glad, mournfully but firmly. She took Ada by the arm. 'Come and meet Darren.'

A goat was standing on the stage of the third carriage chewing the corner of a copy of the *Observer of London*.

'Open this anywhere and ask Darren anything,' said Vlad, handing Ada the newspaper.

Ada opened the paper. 'What is the circumference of the Prince Regent's trousers?' she asked.

'Baaa . . . sixty-four inches . . . Baaa!' replied Darren. Ada was impressed.

'Step this way,' said Vlad, taking Ada to the fourth carriage, the one marked 'Private – Keep

Out'. The door opened, and Lord Sydney Whimsy stepped out, followed by Maxim de Trumpet-Oil the painter and Heston Harboil the cook.

'Very punctual, Miss Goth,' said Lord Sydney. 'In our line of work, timing is everything.'

'Your line of work,'

repeated Ada. 'You mean organizing fetes . . .'

'In a manner of speaking.' Lord Sydney smiled. 'We are secret agents, Miss Goth,' he told her, 'on His Regent's Secret Service. These are agents 001 to 004 –' he nodded to the Glum-Stokers – 'and Heston and Maxim are 005 and 006. I, myself, am . . .'

'Baaa . . . 007 . . . Baaa!' said Darren the memory goat.

'Indeed,' said Lord Sydney.

Ada swallowed. 'And you need *my* help?' she said.

Chapter Eleven

arylebone took off her spectacles and polished them agitatedly on her apron. She put them back on her nose, then grasped Ada's hand in both paws.

'Lord Sydney is depending on me,' said Ada. 'I can't let him down!'

It was the day of the Full-Moon Fete, or, to be exact, the night. The moon had risen, bright and round, and was casting its silvery light over the house and grounds of Ghastly-Gorm Hall, but there was still no sign of Lord Goth. In a few hours it would be Ada's birthday, and as none of the Attic Club had mentioned it when she'd let them in on Lord Sydney's plan earlier in the day, she assumed they'd forgotten. But now she had something far more important to think about.

Ada straightened her red cape and picked up her fencing umbrella.

'How do I look?' she asked.

But Marylebone had already retreated into the depths of the wardrobe.

Glancing over at her eight-poster bed, Ada saw a neat little parcel wrapped in striped paper and tied with a ribbon sitting on her bedspread.

'You remembered!' she said.

A low growl came from the wardrobe.

When Ada got outside she heard the crunch of carriage wheels on gravel and looking down the drive she saw her father coming towards her!

He was riding his hobby horse, Pegasus. There was a lady sitting behind him in the saddle, clutching him tightly by the waist.

They were followed up the drive by Lord Goth's elegant touring carriage pulled by two chestnut horses.

Lord Goth drew up at the bottom of the steps

and climbed off Pegasus. 'Ada!' he exclaimed, throwing his arms wide. 'Father!' Ada ran down the steps and threw herself into Lord Goth's arms. 'It's so good to have you home,' she said, hugging him tightly. 'It's good to *be* home,' said Lord Goth. 'I had to take a detour to meet a sailing ship at Liverpool, but I've made it back in time for the Full-Moon Fete.'

He turned and helped his companion off the hobby horse, which was wheeled away by two grooms.

'This is my friend Lady Caroline Lambchop,' said Lord Goth. 'We met on the banks of Lake

Windermere and seem to have become inseparable ever since.'

'So you're Lord Goth's little girl,' said Lady Caroline Lambchop. 'How enchanting you look in your red cape.' She gave a tinkling laugh and Ada saw her father wince.

'I've said that Lady Caroline can help me judge the Great Ghastly-Gorm Bake Off, whatever that is.' Lord Goth shrugged. 'Some foolish idea of Sydney's. Maltravers has been organizing it.'

Ada smiled knowingly.

'Then Lady Caroline has promised to go back to her book group and leave me in peace!' Lord Goth said, and sighed heavily.

'Oh, Goth, you're such a tease!' exclaimed Lady Caroline, seizing his hand and refusing to let go.

Just then, there came the most extraordinary sound. It was as if a donkey was having its tail put through a mangle while a cat on a hot tin roof was chased by a wheezing ox.

'The Gormless Quire!' said Ada. 'Right on time!'

'I suppose we'd better get on with it,' said Lord Goth without enthusiasm.

Coming along the drive were four men in straw top hats playing unlikely instruments as they walked.

Behind them came three large ladies singing a midsummer carol called 'Hot King Wenceslas'. The villagers of Gormless followed behind, holding flaming torches and joining in the singing every so often, then forgetting the words. Last came a group of men with blue-painted faces and straw skirts that reached down to their ankles. They were balancing pillowcases stuffed with straw on their heads and pulling a large wicker basket on wheels in the shape of an oblong sheep. The basket was full of chestnuts.

'How adorably rustic!' simpered Lady Caroline Lambchop.

The group gathered around the bandstand beneath 'Old Hardy' as the full moon shone down on the dear-deer park. The Gormless Quire

settled themselves on the bandstand and then
began to play a fast and furious tune while the
three large ladies sang 'Once in Royal Tunbridge
Wells'.

All at once the crowd parted, and the men with
blue faces stepped forward. They formed two
rows and, in time to the music, began hitting each
other over the head with the pillowcases.

This went on until all the pillowcases were empty. Then the quire played 'While Shepherds Washed Their Socks by Night' and the crowd gathered in a large circle while Lord Goth took a flaming torch and set fire to the wicker lamb.

The villagers danced around the burning basket until the fire reduced it to ashes, then they ate the roasted chestnuts.* Ada's chestnut tasted delicious.

'Thank goodness that's over for another year,' Lord Goth whispered to Ada with a little smile.

'There's still the raffle,' Ada reminded him.

'And those delicious cakes!' squealed Lady Caroline. 'It's just too exciting for words!'

On the steps of Ghastly-Gorm Hall, the Twee Raffelites had set

Webbed Foot Notes

*Roasting chestnuts at the full moon fete replaced roasting dormice, which was considered cruel and they didn't taste as nice.

up their easels, each holding a painting under a cloth. The villagers formed an orderly queue while J.M.W. Turnip sold raffle tickets.

When everyone, including Ada, Lord Goth and Lady Caroline Lambchop, had bought one, J.M.W. Turnip invited each painter to unveil their masterpiece.

Stubby George pulled the dust sheet from his easel to reveal a painting of Lord Goth's Lincoln Green Armchair.

Instead of Sir Stephen Belljar, Stubby George had painted a hobby-horse groom holding the

Lincoln Armchair by the handlebars. The groom looked a lot like Arthur Halford.

Next Romney Marsh revealed his painting. The villagers broke into wild applause.

Then Maxim de Trumpet-Oil pulled off the dust sheet covering the small painting Ada had seen him working on at the Alpine Gnome Rockery. Beside her, Ada heard Lord Goth chuckle. The painting was so realistic it looked as if you could reach into the picture and pick the gnome up.

'Old Stumpy – I've taken plenty of potshots at him.' He smiled.

'So it's true what they say about you,' giggled Lady Caroline. 'You *are* mad, bad and dangerous to gnomes.'

Sir Stephen Belljar clip-clopped forward and did an excited clog dance on the steps before whipping off the sheet covering his most famous satirical print with a flourish.

THE GREAT CUMBERLAND SAUSAGE AT HIS NEW PLEASURE PALACE IN BRIGHTON

'Quite scandalous!' exclaimed Lady Caroline, clinging on to Lord Goth's arm.

Finally J.M.W. Turnip stepped up and revealed his canvas.

'It's called *Soot, Steam and Slowness — the Steam-Traction Carnival*,' he announced.

There was a burst of excited applause. It was coming from Emily Cabbage, who was standing at the foot of the steps.

'Tickets at the ready. Miss Emily Cabbage will now draw the first ticket . . .' Turnip announced to the crowd.

He carefully took off his extremely tall hat and gave it a good shake before motioning for Emily to dip her hand inside. She reached in and pulled out a raffle-ticket stub.

'Seven, eight, five, six, four . . .' Emily read out the extremely long number.

There was a long pause while everyone looked at their tickets, then several people claimed to have won, only to discover they'd misheard the numbers and Emily had to read them over several times. It all took rather a long time. Finally, after quite a few attempts, Bathsheba Ambridge of the Gormless Quire won, and chose Stubby George's painting of the oblong sheep, making the rest of the villagers extremely jealous. The other winners were a kitchen maid, who chose the Alpine Gnome, one of the hobby-horse grooms, who chose the Lincoln Armchair, and another member of the quire, Gabriel Acorn, who played the sagbutt and who chose the satirical print.

Finally there was only one ticket to be called and one painting remaining. Emily dipped her hand into the hat, pulled out a stub and read out the number.

'Mine!' exclaimed Lady Caroline Lambchop, jumping up and down in excitement. Lord Goth had bought her raffle ticket on the condition that she let go of his hand. She pushed her way through the crowd with surprising strength for such a slight figure and grasped J.M.W. Turnip's carnival painting. She returned to Ada and her father.

'What a dreadful daub! Here –' Lady Caroline fluttered her eyelashes at Lord Goth as she handed the painting to Ada – 'you take it, my dear.'

Just then Maltravers appeared in the doorway of the hall. He smiled a dusty smile as he pointed in the direction of the drawing-room garden. 'The Great Ghastly-Gorm Bake Off is about to begin!' he announced.

Chapter Twelve

verybody trooped along the gravel path, past the front of the east wing and round the back to the drawing-room garden. When they got there they found the Transylvanian Steam-Traction Carnival in full swing. The bat circus was doing loop-the loops, the shy coconuts were bobbing up and down in their mahogany cups, taking bashful peeks at the crowd, and Darren the memory goat was chewing thoughtfully on the literary pages of the *Observer of London* newspaper. The Glum-Stokers were lined up, staring miserably at the approaching people. Ada noticed that the leader of the 'Dorris Men' glanced over at them and winked meaningfully.

'A madding crowd, if ever I saw one,' said Glad gloomily.

'Move along. Bake off, in the Spiegel tent, that way,' called Vlad in a monotonous voice. 'All the fun of the fair, this way.'

Most of the crowd, Ada included, went into the Spiegel tent, though a few turned and walked over to the carnival. The Ambridge sisters were very taken with the bat circus, clapping their hands and exclaiming in musical voices that they'd never seen the like.

Ada glanced back as she stepped through the doors of the Spiegel tent.

Kingsley and Arthur Halford were

lingering in front of Darren the memory goat, whistling tunefully.

Inside the Spiegel tent, a hundred decoratively framed mirrors reflected back the faces of the excited villagers of Gormless and the servants of Ghastly-Gorm Hall. Ada followed her father and Lady Caroline Lambchop up on to a raised stage in the centre of the tent, beneath the dome, with its large mirrorball and octagonal openings through which she could see a brilliant white full moon.

'Make way for the contestants of the Great Ghastly-Gorm Bake Off! Maltravers's wheezing voice sounded over the heads of the crowd.

The outdoor butler held open the double doors as the cooks entered, each carrying a large plate on which their creation was magnificently displayed.

There were 'oohs' and 'aahs' from the crowd and a shrill 'Be still, my beating heart!' from Lady Caroline, as the cooks approached the stage and carefully laid their plates on the long trestle table in front of Lord Goth.

Mary Huckleberry had baked a Young Victoria sponge with white chocolate fondant in the shape of the Prince Regent's new pavilion in Brighton. She handed a large cake knife to her manservant, Hollyhead, who cut two slices and presented them to Lady Caroline and Lord Goth.

BRIGHTON PAVILION CAKE

'Good texture,' said Lord Goth.

'It speaks to me of sunshine and decadence!' exclaimed Lady Caroline. 'No wonder his trousers are so big!'

Hollyhead cut slices from his own cake, a

Liverpool strawberry
roll with a spun-sugar
cormorant on top.

'Good texture,'
said Lord Goth.

'The Liver bird
is just too precious
for words!' trilled Lady

LIVERPOOL STRAWBERRY ROLL

Caroline, spitting cake crumbs in her excitement.
'This has all the bustle and roll of a great seaport!'

The Hairy Hikers looked on nervously from
behind their long shaggy beards as Lord Goth and
Lady Caroline tasted
their giant Geordie
scone with black-and-
white chocolate ganache.

'Good texture,' said
Lord Goth.

GIANT GEORDIE SCONE

'Wild, rugged!' breathed
Lady Caroline, fluttering her eyes at Lord Goth,
'and unutterably handsome.'

'It's so wonderful to finally meet you, Lord Goth,' said Nigellina Sugarspoon, handing him an extra-large slice of her giant fondant fancy with praline-spoon decorations.

GIANT FONDANT FANCY

'Charmed, dear lady,' said Lord Goth, 'the texture is really very good.'

'Rather dry,' said Lady Caroline, 'in my opinion.'

Gordon Ramsgate frowned furiously as Lord Goth and Lady Caroline tasted his 'Nightmare in the Kitchen' cake covered in white chilli-chocolate with marzipan figures.

'Please don't be upset,' cooed Lady Caroline. 'Yours is a magnificent and fiery vision . . .'

'Oh, I'm not cross,' said

'NIGHTMARE' IN THE KITCHEN' CAKE

Gordon Ramsgate with an even more furious frown. 'I always look like this.'

'Good texture,' said Lord Goth.

William Flake handed Ruby the outer-pantry maid the cake knife.

'You cut the first slice, my dear.' He smiled as he stroked Tyger-Tyger. 'After all, you've been such a tremendous help.'

Ruby blushed with pride as she cut two slices of William Flake's Jerusalem cake with its fondant footprint on green icing sugar.

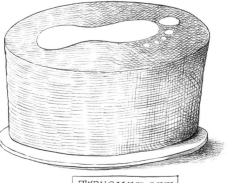

JERUSALEM CAKE

'And did those bakers in ancient times bake upon England's pastures green?' mused Lady Caroline. Lord Goth rolled his eyes.

'Good texture,' he said.

Finally they came to Heston Harboil, at the end of the trestle table.

His creation was larger than all the rest and rather disappointingly decorated with yellow gloop.

"PLUM PUDDING IN DANGER" CAKE

'This is my "Plum Pudding in Danger" cake,' said Heston, 'with gas-proof custard.'

Beside him, Pushkin the fat Muscovy duck nodded in agreement.

Just then there was a loud whining howl and the double doors to the Spiegel tent burst open.

Two enormous poodles, one white, the other black, bounded into the tent followed by the Grocers of the Night, Didier Dangle and Gerard Dopplemousse and their balloonist, Madame Grand Gousier.

'Everybody stay just where they are!' she commanded as the poodles slammed the doors shut and stood guard in front of them.

'The Full-Moon Fete is cancelled!' she cackled . . .

Chapter Thirteen

he Grocers of
the Night
and their
balloonist
raised their
black
capes
and
flapped up into the air, swooping over the heads
of the terrified crowd and circling the cooks at
the trestle table.

Lady Caroline Lambchop fainted and had
to be caught by Lord Goth as the three figures
closed in.

'What do you want with us?' Lord Goth
demanded, his brooding eyes alight with anger.

Didier Dangle landed at one end of the

trestle, Gerard Dopplemousse at the other, as
Madame Grand Gousier came lightly down to earth
in front of Lord Goth.
The cooks cowered
behind him.
Ada edged
towards the
end of the
table, her
umbrella
gripped
firmly
in her
hand.
Glancing in the mirrors, she saw
that the grocers had no reflections.
'We simply want to drink the
blood of the finest cooks in England,
because it is the most delicious,' said
Madame Grand Gousier with a smile
that revealed her white, pointed teeth.

'We are, how you say . . . ? Gourmet Vampires.'
Didier Dangle grinned, eyeing Nigellina
Sugarspoon.

'We drink the blood of chefs, and only the best
will do,' explained Gerard Dopplemousse, leering
hungrily at the Hairy Hikers.

'But since you are standing in our way,'
Madame Grand Gousier said with a sinister smile,
'we shall start with you!'

'Now, Ada!' the leader of the Dorris Men
shouted from the midst of the cowering crowd.

Ada jumped up on to the table and danced
deftly around the Brighton Pavilion,
nimbly stepped over the spun-sugar
cormorant on the Liverpool
roll and dodged the giant
   Geordie scone.

With a scream of outrage, Madame
Grand Gousier grabbed at Ada's
ankles and missed, sending the
praline spoons on the giant
fondant fancy
flying.

Ada swerved past the 'Nightmare in the Kitchen' cake and used the fondant footprint on the Jerusalem cake as a stepping stone to avoid Didier Dangle's grasp.

She leaped down to the end of the table and forced Gerard Dopplemousse back with the tip of her fencing umbrella.

'Seize the little Goth girl!' screamed Madame Grand Gousier at the Grocers of the Night. The vampires closed in. Ada twirled the fencing umbrella in her hand and then lunged forward, plunging the point deep into Heston Harboil's 'Plum Pudding in Danger' cake with gas-proof custard. As she pulled

it out again there was a loud hiss
and a cloud of pungent fumes filled
the air.

'Garlic gas,' said Heston proudly. Pushkin
nodded from Heston's hat, where he'd taken refuge.

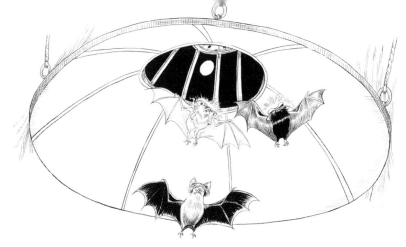

'Nooooo!' screeched the vampires, shrinking back as the garlic gas filled the Spiegel tent.

'Yes!' said the leader of the Dorris Men, wiping the blue paint off his face with the corner of the trestle tablecloth, revealing himself as none other than Lord Sydney.

Holding their noses, the three gourmet vampires launched themselves up into the air, transforming themselves into bats as they did so.

Ada stared up at the three black shapes flapping towards the openings at the top of the tent.

There followed three loud CLUNKS as each bat hit its head against Maxim de Trumpet-Oil's latest masterpiece, hanging horizontally below the ceiling. It was a perfectly realistic painting of the top of the tent on a circular oak panel.

'I call it *The Illusion of Escape,*' said Maxim modestly.

Emily and the Twee Raffelites broke into applause.

Lord Sydney Whimsy held out his pillowcase and caught the falling bats one after the other, then tied the pillowcase shut with a flourish. The Dorris Men broke into a cheer.

Two loud whines filled the air and all heads turned towards the doors of the tent.

Belle and Sebastian had looked up from the pile of toasted marshmallows they'd been guzzling to find two stout leather collars round their necks. Kingsley held the lead to one, and Arthur had the other. They took a bow as the whole tent gave loud 'hurrahs'.

'I'm sorry, Lord Goth, but nothing could persuade me to stay another moment!' came Lady Caroline Lambchop's indignant voice.

Lord Goth held out a hand and helped Ada down from the table. 'My brave little daughter,' he said, ignoring Lady Caroline. 'Your mother would have been so proud.'

'Get out of my way!' Lady Caroline exclaimed as she barged a path through the villagers and stormed out of the Spiegel tent.

'On behalf of His Regent's Secret Service,' said Lord Sydney, 'I'd like to thank you, Ada, and your friends in the Attic Club.'

Kingsley and

Arthur nodded and smiled, and William Cabbage, who'd gone completely unnoticed, fed Belle and Sebastian some more marshmallows.

Ruby the outer-pantry maid, who'd had quite a scare, wiped her eyes on her apron. Emily, who was shaking Maxim de Trumpet-Oil's hand, looked over and smiled. 'I'll take the poodles,' said Maltravers, reaching out to take the leads

from Arthur and Kingsley. He glanced over at Lord Goth. 'If that's all right with you, My Lord?'

Lord Goth nodded. 'Lord Sydney says you've been most helpful, Maltravers, thank you.'

The outdoor butler bowed, then led Belle and Sebastian out of the tent, followed by Lord Sydney, Ada and the rest of the Attic Club.

'What about them?' Ada asked, pointing to the shapes battling to get out of the knotted pillowcase in Lord Sydney's arms.

'We'll take care of things,' said the Glum-Stokers, rather more cheerfully than usual, as they met them outside.

Vlad took the pillowcase and handed it to Glad, who put it in the fourth carriage of the Steam-Traction Carnival and locked the door.

'Dangle, Dopplemousse and Grand Gousier – last of the notorious Vampire Gang . . . We've been trying to catch them for years,' said Lord Sydney, with satisfaction. 'The operation's code-named . . .'

'Baaa . . . the thirty-nine crêpes . . . Baaa!' said Darren the memory goat.

'The Glum-Stokers will take them to a home for delinquent vampires,' Lord Sydney continued, 'in an obscure coastal village called Eastbourne.'

'If you'll excuse me' he said, with an elegant bow, 'there is just one thing left to organize.' He turned on his heels and disappeared back inside the Spiegel tent. Just then the clock above the hobby-horse stables struck midnight.

'It's my birthday!' said Ada.

'I know' said Lord Goth, waving two grooms over. They were wheeling a beautiful bicycle between them. Ada couldn't believe her eyes.

'Usually nobody remembers my birthday except Marylebone,' she said.

'That will change from now on,' said Lord Goth. 'This is my birthday present to you. She's called Little Pegasus. A hobby pony,' he added with a smile.

'And I painted a birthday card,' said Emily.

'And we all signed it,' said Kingsley.

Inside the Spiegel tent the Gormless Quire began a low chorus of 'For She's a Jolly Good Marshmallow' and Lord Sydney stuck his head out of the tent and waved everyone inside. There on the raised table was the most magnificent cake Ada had ever seen.

'All the cooks helped,' said Mrs Beat'em, smiling broadly.

'I made the figure on top out of spun sugar,' said Ruby shyly. 'Mr Harboil helped me.'

Ada was about to thank everybody when she felt a tap on her shoulder and turning round saw Marylebone standing before her, another birthday present in her paws. Behind her large spectacles Marylebone's eyes brimmed with tears. She held out the neatly wrapped parcel and Ada opened it.

'Fencing gloves!' she exclaimed. Ada rushed into Marylebone's arms. 'They're lovely, but coming out of the wardrobe is the best present you could give me!' she said, hugging her.

There was a little growl, as if someone was clearing their throat, and the smallest of the Dorris Men stepped through the crowd as the choir sang 'In the Bright Midsummer'.

Ada stepped back as the figure pulled off its grass skirt and broad-brimmed hat to reveal itself as a short, stout, spectacled bear of military bearing.

'General Simon Batholiver,' Ada breathed.

Epilogue

da knocked quietly on Lucy Borgia's bedroom door.

'Come in,' said her governess softly.

Ada entered the small room in the turret at the top of the great dome of Ghastly-Gorm Hall. Her governess was lying on her bed. She looked very sad.

That evening, just after sunset, Lord Goth, Ada and Lucy had stood on the rooftops of Ghastly-Gorm Hall and waved as the hot-air balloon rose into the night sky. From the basket, Marylebone, General Simon Batholiver and Lord Sydney Whimsy had waved back.

'Parting is such sweet sorrow,' Lord Sydney had called to Lucy, 'but unavoidable, I'm afraid, in my line of work.'

The Steam-
Traction
Carnival
had left,
the
Spiegel
tent had
been
taken
down
and loaded
back on to
the Cumbrian
juggernaut, and

the cooks had departed with it, together with the
painters in their stagecoach. Ghastly-Gorm Hall
was returning to normal. There was a meeting of
the Attic Club, and a new edition of *The Chimney
Pot* to prepare, but first Ada had wanted to see
how Lucy Borgia was.

'Your lady's maid and her general will catch a sailing ship from Liverpool. Then Lord Sydney says he has urgent business elsewhere.' Lucy sighed. 'Who knows when we'll see him at Ghastly-Gorm Hall again. I did so enjoy helping him with his plan to catch those awful grocers – they

give us vampires a bad name. I'm just sorry I couldn't have been there to see it, but, of course, the garlic . . .'

She sat up and looked out of the window. There was no reflection in the dark glass and Ada saw her dark eyes take on a sad, faraway look.

'He did so remind me of that young painter I knew, so long ago, the one who painted my portrait . . . It's at times like this I wish I could see it again . . .'

'I know,' said Ada, with a smile, 'which is why I brought you this.'

THE MONA LUCY

LINCOLN GREEN HOBBY HORSE

OLD STUMPY

BAA BAA WHITE SHEEP

SOOT, STEAM AND SLOWNESS – THE STEAM-TRACTION CARNIVAL

This is a fine
Sizzle, is it not?

I fear the
fabric will not
hold your highness

THE GREAT CUMBERLAND SAUSAGE AT HIS NEW
PLEASURE PALACE IN BRIGHTON

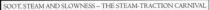

STILL LIFE WITH A MOUSE

'THE' 1ST LORD GOTH

THE 2ND LORD GOTH

NARCISSUS AND DIANA

THE 3RD LORD GOTH

THE EMPRESS OF GORM

DIANA, DUCHESS OF GHASTLESHIRE
AND HER SPANIEL ACTON

THE 4TH LORD GOTH

GIRL WITH A PEARL EARRING

BOY WITH FRUIT ON HIS HEAD

THE 5TH LORD GOTH

Bring me my bowl of burning gold,
Bring me my spatulas of desire,
Bring me my whisk, and logs untold,
To fuel my chariot of fire!

William Flake's 'Jerusalem'

CHARIOT
OF
FIRE

INNOCENCE AND EXPERIENCE

JERUSALEM CAKE

Ode to a Nightingale
SOUP
WITH AUTUMN FUMES AND OVER WORKING FIRE
Complements of
HESTON HARBOIL

Shall I compare Thee to
A Summer's Trifle
BREAKFAST BRIOCHE WITH STILTON
SOLAR FLARES
Complements of
HESTON HARBOIL

CHOCOLATE FINGER LICKING
UPSIDE DOWN CAKE

GIANT 'GEORDIE' SCONE

BRIGHTON PAVILION CAKE

'PLUM PUDDING IN DANGER' CAKE

A CAIRN OF CUMBRIAN
MACAROONS

GIANT FONDANT FANCY

LIVERPOOL STRAWBERRY ROLL

'NIGHTMARE IN THE KITCHEN' CAKE

EXTREMELY CROSS CROISSANTS
WITH CHILLI PEPPER DUSTING

BABY VICTORIA SPONGES
WITH AN AMUSEMENT OF PLUM JAM

THE PRINCE REGENT
AS AN ECLAIR

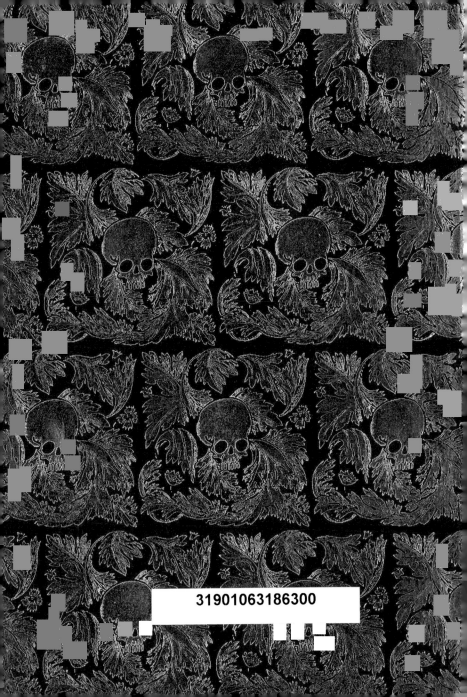

31901063186300